BS 5750/ISO 9000 Made Plain

How to install BS 5750/ISO/9000 in your company

Maxwell Philip

STANLEY
THORNES

First published in 1994 by
Stanley Thornes (Publishers) Ltd
Ellenborough House
Wellington Street
CHELTENHAM
GL50 1YD
UK

A catalogue record for this book is available from the British Library.
ISBN 0 7487 1700 5

Photoset in Linotron Palatino by
Northern Phototypesetting Co, Ltd, Bolton
Printed and bound in Great Britain by
Redwood Books, Wilts

Cover design: Martin Miller

Contents

Part 3 How to consolidate BS 5750/ISO 9000

How to use this book

This book places before you the basis of a Documented Quality System to BS 5750/ISO 9000 whether you operate in the manufacturing industry, the service sector or are engaged in teaching the principles of quality assurance.

As is discussed in the Introduction and Chapter 12, the application of BS 5750/ISO 9000 in the service sector has been comparatively recent, though it is now growing rapidly. If you are in 'service' may we suggest that you go straight to Chapter 12. Reading it will demonstrate both the importance of BS 5750/ISO 9000 to you and issues of particular significance in a service context.

Then pick up the thread from Chapter 1. Quite deliberately, the chapters are arranged in the sequence in which we develop BS 5750/ISO 9000 with a client company: first, an introduction to the Standard; then advice on how to get started, including an action plan for immediate implementation; then preparation and 'activation' of documents and 'generic' procedures (general ones applying to most companies in much the same way); then preparation of the much more specific (and in some ways more demanding) ones defining core activities such as buying, selling, processing (or servicing), design and inspection and testing.

We then examine preparation for assessment and registration to BS 5750/ISO 9000 and what people should know about the actual assessment and its aftermath.

Finally we invite a look beyond BS 5750/ISO 90000 to the concept of Total Quality Management (TQM), for which so much has been claimed, particularly in Japan. We also consider whether a slimmer variant of it, which we call 'Improved Quality Management', might not be more appropriate for British, European and equivalent companies seeking to progress beyond BS 5750/ISO 9000 more rapidly than TQM allows.

The main aim of the book is to enable organisations to 'self start' on BS 5750/ISO 9000 without immediate dependency on consultants. Admittedly, they may need to call on them at some stage but they will be surprised by how far they can progress to BS 5750/ISO 9000 by following this text and, in particular, the guidelines given on page 11. For emphasis we repeat the more pertinent of them here.

1 Make full use of texts such as this one which seek to save you money by placing before you the basis of a complete, conforming Documented Quality System to BS 5750/ISO 9000.

2 Do your best to convert the specimen Quality Manual of Appendix 1 and the procedures provided in the text to the precise needs of your company. Remember that they have to state exactly what happens in *your* organisation. Do not overclaim in any way and do not sweep anything under the carpet.

3 Once this has been completed, you should have a Documented Quality System ready to put into operation. Now review where you stand in regard to BS 5750/ISO 9000. Can you proceed alone from here to assessment? If you consider you can, then you have no apparent need for consultancy assistance.

4 An excellent way of establishing your status against BS 5750/ISO 9000 at this point is to audit your emergent quality system against the checklists provided in Appendix 3. They were devised exactly for that purpose and should soon indicate to you whether you are in control.

5 If you identify a need for consultancy at this stage at least you have already cut costs substantially by having yourself written much of the documentation required by the Standard in your business.

6 Your brief to a consultant then reduces considerably from that of a firm commissioning consultancy services from the beginning. You may be confident enough to proceed with the consultancy on the basis of a short term contract giving then a restricted remit, such as to audit your status against BS 5750/ISO 9000 and to propose remedial measures for faults found.

This book will have succeeded in its intention if it enables companies in the manufacturing and service sectors to proceed to BS 5750/ISO 9000 along the above path at considerably reduced expense.

The author is Senior Partner of Maxwell Philip Associates, Consulting Industrial Chemists, 28 Netherburn Avenue, Glasgow G44 3UF, United Kingdom. The company provides a range of consultancy services, including guidance to BS 5750/ISO 9000 in the manufacturing and service industries.

Author's Note

A slight revision of BS 5750/ISO 9000 was provisionally agreed in 1993 with the view to the revised standard being available during 1994. The revised standard is to be renamed BS EN ISO 9000 with a subtitle in large print: 'FORMERLY BS 5750'. The change is largely one of title, the intention being eventually to phase out reference to BS 5750. Significant amendments to BS 5750/ISO 9000 ('BS EN ISO 9000') are unlikely before 1996 at the earliest.

Part 1 – Introduction

Chapter 1

BS 5750/ISO 9000 – an introduction

1.1   BS 5750: 1987, Parts 1, 2 and 3. An outline

BS 5750 is an officially accredited and externally assessed standard for quality management systems dating from 1979, revised in 1987 and subject to further revision by 1996. Standards have to be met and maintained over a range of areas of control as summarised on page 4 for BS 5750: 1987, Parts 1 and 2.

Initially the major uptake of BS 5750 was by the engineering industry, followed during the 1980s by other manufacturing industries. Around 1990, service based organisations became increasingly aware of the benefits of operating to an externally ratified quality system and the list of registered firms to BS 5750 now includes, for example, a number of solicitors, doctors, colleges of education, car dealerships, and banks. Despite the engineering origins of BS 5750 (still recognisable in the tone of some of the Standard), we consider that it can be effectively adapted to the requirements of service industries on lines proposed in Chapter 12.

There is also a Part 3 of BS 5750 but as Part 3 is for companies who specialise in inspection and testing of finished products, it need concern us no further in this text which is directed to manufacturing and service industry companies providing a service other than final product inspection. Parts 1 and 2 are very similar, the only difference between the two being that Part 1 contains two clauses more than Part 2, which are concerned with design and servicing. 'Servicing' in 'Part 1' refers to a company's arrangements for after sales service – not provision of their total service. Part 1, because it is longer, is somewhat harder to achieve than Part 2 and this is generally reflected in higher assessment and upkeep fees.

To dispel a possible misunderstanding, companies head for

assessment to either Part 1 or Part 2, not both. The one they aim for is determined by the extent to which they are involved in design. As a guide, a company without any individual or section wholly or largely devoted to design, should probably be aiming for Part 2. If you are a borderline case, discuss this with the assessing body of your choice at an early stage. Getting it right at the start could save you time at a later stage.

The twenty clauses of BS 5750: 1987, Part 1 and the eighteen clauses of Part 2' are listed below side by side. It will be noted that the eighteen clauses common to both versions are identical.

The clause headings of BS 5750, Parts 1 and 2

Standards of performance and documentation have to be set for each of the undermentioned areas of control of companies' operations. Later we examine each clause in detail and explain how to respond to them in typical businesses. For the moment it is sufficient simply to list them.

Part 1	Part 2	Clause heading
4.1	4.1	Management responsibility
4.2	4.2	Quality system
4.3	4.3	Contract review
4.4	N/A	Design control
4.5	4.4	Document control
4.6	4.5	Purchasing
4.8	4.7	Product identification and traceability
4.9	4.8	Process control
4.10	4.9	Inspection and testing
4.11	4.10	Inspection measuring and test equipment
4.12	4.11	Inspection and test status
4.13	4.12	Control of nonconforming product
4.14	4.13	Corrective action
4.15	4.14	Handling storage, packaging and delivery
4.16	4.15	Quality records
4.17	4.16	Internal quality audits
4.18	4.17	Training
4.19	N/A	Servicing
4.20	4.18	Statistical techniques

Advantages of BS 5750

These are the ones we have most frequently encountered in our dealings with firms. There are others and you can, no doubt, supply some of them from your own experience.

1 Supplier and subcontractor performance is improved through regular monitoring.
2 Processes and services are systematically audited, reviewed and recorded.
3 Relations with customers are improved, some of whom may demand BS 5750 compliance as a condition of trading.
4 A statement of official registration to BS 5750 and the use of the BS 5750 logo on companies' literature and vans are decided market advantages.
5 Possible opening of new markets. We have seen examples of new business opening within days of registration to BS 5750.
6 Reduced likelihood of losing existing market share. Under the single market, British firms are open to face to face competition from firms in all member countries. Even such traditional home markets as milk marketing and urban cleaning services are already the subject of such competition.
7 Possible mitigation of risk from customer complaints and claims through demonstrable attention to 'Due Diligence'.
8 European and general export marketing are facilitated through ISO 9000 and EN 29000 which are international equivalents of BS 5750 and are conferred along with BS 5750 at no extra charge.
9 Registration with a major assessing body such as BSI Quality Assurance as a BS 5750 company means that the company is listed on their buyers' guide, with improved marketing prospects.
10 BS 5750 registration is essential for companies seeking additional quality or marketing seals of approval such as the Kitemark (which is a *product* validation).
11 Customers recognise that an externally assessed quality assurance system such as BS 5750 is a considerable achievement and respond accordingly.
12 Once a firm has earned BS 5750, it is well positioned to extend its principles to other areas of its business, such as financial control and marketing, taking a decisive stride towards Total Quality Management (TQM).

1.3   Reasons for *not* going for BS 5750

It is rare to meet a firm which having achieved BS 5750, regretted the time and effort. However it is advisable that companies consider the possible disadvantages of installing BS 5750 in their organisation before committing themselves to it. Generally the advantages outweigh the disadvantages but not always and it is well to examine some reasons for *not* embarking on BS 5750.

1 Your product or service is provided locally to small customers to whom BS 5750 would not be as important as maintenance of the quality of product or service you provide to them. Note the word 'small'. If your customers are large (and therefore likely to be aware of, or even registered to BS 5750) a case for considering BS 5750 begins to emerge, even if your customers are local.
2 Cost. BS 5750 is not cheap to instal (see Section 2.2). Be sure that your outlay has a high likelihood of being recouped by increased business.
3 You already hold alternative, externally validated, accreditations of at least similar status to BS 5750, for example, your pharmaceutics factory is approved by the Medicines Control Agency; your quality system for food production is endorsed by your principal customers even although not to BS 5750; or your consultancy service is verified and listed by a body controlling your operational standards. Note, however, that even such valuable credentials may not secure you certain contracts if there is an insistence on BS 5750 by the prospective customer.
4 Bureaucracy. BS 5750 is a *documented* quality system. Medium to large firms can handle the documentation comfortably. So can most small firms. But to a two man joinery working to a deadline, the documentation can be a burden even given an efficient office back-up. Be sure you can handle the paperwork before committing yourself to BS 5750.
5 Resources. Even in the smallest firm you should allow up to 'half a person' to control BS 5750 documentation in the busy period leading up to assessment. This could amount to a rather overworked secretary for some months, with the reward of a more interesting job after the firm is registered to BS 5750. There is also a management commitment, for discussion later. If you rely on a typewriter you may also consider it worthwhile to operate a word processor (WP) as it is much easier to store, update and reissue documents with the WP (see Chapter 4.5).

You may also have to pay for additional services to meet certain requirements of BS 5750, for example, the services of calibration engineers could prove necessary to validate your gauges if you are in precision engineering and not already fully meeting the BS 5750 requirement for traceable instrument calibration. You may also have to allocate space for storage of BS 5750 related documents.

6 Company culture. A small firm might be totally resistant to all but the basic essential trading documents such as invoices, purchase forms and accounting records. Some perfectly good companies operate profitably in exactly this manner and they should not lightly discard a system that works.

1.4   BS 5750 and the ISO 9000 (and EN 29000) series

For all practical purposes, BS 5750, ISO 9000 and EN 29000 are one and the same thing by different names. When a company gains registration to BS 5750: 1987, Part 1 (for example), it automatically acquires ISO 9001 and EN 29001 at no extra cost. There are identical arrangements for Parts 2 and 3 of BS 5750.

EN 29000 is significant within Europe and ISO 9000 has world wide relevance and both titles may be more readily identifiable than BS 5750 by overseas customers or suppliers of British companies. There are obvious benefits in this for firms with an actual or potential export business.

As the equivalence of these systems has become more widely understood it is now common to see reference to extended titles such as BS 5750 Part 1/ISO 9001 and BS 5750 Part 1/ISO 9001/EN 29001.

In this text the term BS 5750 is generally preferred as it is more readily recognised by small companies in the UK rather than ISO 9000. Periodically, for example, in the chapter headings, the dual title BS 5750/ISO 9000 is used as reminder that BS 5750 and ISO 9000 are equivalent. Although there is a growing use of ISO 9000 on its own in some quarters we have avoided this in the text as a possible source of confusion.

1.5   The future development of BS 5750

BS 5750 is not a static system and is subject to on-going review. For example, the Standard was issued in 1979 and reviewed in 1987. The 1987 version is likely to be current until 1995/1996 when it is scheduled for reissue in light of developments since 1987. These have included the widespread adoption of BS 5750 by manu-facturers in industries other than engineering (which once was the primary focus of BS 5750) and by a wide range of service companies, including many in the public sector, now open to compulsory competitive tendering.

There has also been a growing uptake of BS 5750/ISO 9000 systems by overseas companies. Controlling bodies in industries such as food, pharmaceutics and orthopaedics have adopted many of the principles of BS 5750 to their quality directives and convergence of their own systems with the BS 5750 system is imminent or actual in some instances.

Moreover, since 1990, BS 5750 Part 2 registration has also been available to 'stockists' (companies who store and supply customers with stock manufactured by other companies). Till then stockists had to be registered under a previous scheme (the BSI Registered Stockist Scheme).

1.6   Related quality matters

The Kitemark

Some small firms confuse the Kitemark with BS 5750. BS 5750 is a quality standard addressing how a company controls its affairs across the range of clauses contained in BS 5750 (see Section 1.2). Registration to BS 5750 signifies that a company has satisfied the criteria of an official assessing body for its operation against those clauses. BS 5750 is not a *product* approval and the Registered Firm Symbol conferred to qualifying firms must not be displayed on or in association with Product or Service or their packaging. Registered firms who wish to make reference to their registration in association with their product may only do so by prior agreement with the Director of their assessing body and then only in line with a prescribed statement.

Kitemark *is* a product approval awarded after rigorous verification of the product's performance against stipulated criteria. A precondition of Kitemark product approval is registration of the manufacturing company to BS 5750.

Guides to BS 5750

BS 4778

This provides guidance on international terms used in quality assurance in the form of a 'quality vocabulary'.

BS 5750, Part 0

This document consists of two sections. The first provides guidance on selection and use of an appropriate quality system, with special reference to the ISO 9001 to 9004 series. The second section addresses the wider subject of development and implementation of quality systems in general.

BS 5750, Part 4

This is a guide to the implementation of BS 5750 in companies.

BS 5750, Part 8
This provides an insight into quality management and quality system elements for services.

BS 5750, Part 13

This affords guidance on application of ISO 9001 to computer software development, supply and maintenance.

The missing numbers in the above series BS 5750 Parts 0 to 13, that is Parts 5, 6, 7, 9, 10, 11 and 12, represent further prospective guides, some of which were previously issued then withdrawn from circulation, while others have yet to be finalised and issued. Should companies purchase some or all of the above BS 5750 addenda to help them implement BS 5750? In our opinion small firms need not buy them, with the exception of Part 13 which is a recommended purchase for small and large firms involved with computer software at the design and development level.

Otherwise, it is more important for an adviser or consultant on BS 5750 to be familiar with these publications and to carry their implications over into their clients' quality system. Companies should however purchase a copy of BS 5750: 1987, Part 1 or Part 2, according to their needs.

Guidance notes on BS 5750

The major assessing bodies to BS 5750 have collaborated to produce excellent free or nominally priced guidance notes on the application of BS 5750/ISO 9000 to a range of manufacturing and service industries such as the Food and Drink Industry, the Pharmaceutical Industry and the Transportation, Storage and Distribution Industries. These slim documents, generally of only ten or so pages, briefly examine each clause of BS 5750 and explain its impact on the industry concerned. Their language is plain and clear and the documents are an invaluable bridge between the rather legalistic language of BS 5750 and the operational requirements of companies aiming for BS 5750 registration.

BS 7750

This is a specification for environmental management systems which was finalised in 1992 to meet a growing requirement for close control of environmental matters under such legal instruments as the *Environmental Protection Act* 1990 and the *Controlled Waste Regulations* 1991. The standard is designed to enable any organisation to establish an effective management system for both sound environmental performance and participation in environmental auditing schemes.

BS 7750 shares common management system principles with BS 5750. Companies with a significant environmental involvement may elect to use BS 5750 as their basic control system and embody the additional environmental requirements of BS 7750 into it. Alternatively they may meet their environmental requirements by installing a quality management system conforming to BS 7750.

BS 7850

Parts 1 and 2 of BS 7850, Total Quality Management, were published in 1992.

Part 1, Guide to management principles, is aimed at chief executives whose support is essential to drive TQM. Its main principles recognise that customer satisfaction, health and safety, environmental considerations and business objectives are mutually dependent and are part of the overall quality objective of a firm.

Part 2, Quality improvement methods, deals with implementation of a continuous quality improvement process and views every aspect of an organisation as a process.

A short guide to development of BS 5750 towards TQM, based on the writer's experience, is given in Chapter 15.

Part 2 – How to install BS 5750/ISO 9000

Chapter 2

Getting started

Contents of chapter:

2.1   Staff implications

BS 5750 requires appointment of a management representative who 'irrespective of other responsibilities, shall have defined authority and responsibility for ensuring that the requirements of this international Standard are implemented and maintained'. Although not stated in the Standard there is also an implied requirement for a deputy to the management representative to maintain continuity of the quality service. Companies already operating a formal quality assurance system frequently appoint their Quality Manager as management representative. There is much to be said for appointing a senior executive, for example, the Managing Director, or the Chief Executive, such as the Chairman or equivalent, to the deputy role, thus ensuring demonstrable commitment to the quality programme at the most senior level.

Therefore neither the Management Representative (MR for present purposes) nor the Deputy (DMR) is normally an additional appointment to a company's payroll. They are additional duties assigned to managers already on the payroll. Possible exceptions to this generalisation could be multinational companies or large corporations in the public sector whose scale might justify appointment of an MR dedicated exclusively to maintenance of the BS 5750 system on a group-wide basis.

Installation and development of the BS 5750 system is a particularly busy period for the MR who should therefore be allocated time away from normal duties to attend to BS 5750 affairs. In our experience this ranges from about a day per week in small firms to close to full-time secondment from normal duties in large ones in the run up to assessment. Installation and development may take as little as three to six months in a company committed to rapid progress to BS 5750, to a year or longer in companies preferring a steadier approach.

During this phase other members of staff will require training for BS 5750, for example, in internal quality auditing, document control and corrective action procedures. Normally this is handled by short-term training courses without major disruption of production or service with personnel returning to normal duties on completion of training. Document control can however be a sizeable on-going task and the case for appointing a part or full time document controller should be evaluated and if necessary provided for. This aspect is discussed in more detail in Section 4.3.

After registration, the time required by the MR and DMR to oversee and maintain the BS 5750 quality system (and for their colleagues to handle their own inputs to the system) should reduce considerably and merge into normal duties.

As a general guide, most small to medium size companies appear to cope with the entire BS 5750 programme, without a single additional appointment, by simply working harder on quality matters, to the benefit of the company.

2.2   Cost implications

Some small firms have the idea that registration to BS 5750 is quite cheap, on the lines of renewing a TV licence, and may well be deterred from proceeding to BS 5750 once they learn the total cost of the project. Partly this reflects a tendency of assessing bodies' fee scales to be in general skewed in favour of larger companies. A two person joinery turning over £100 000 p.a. and heading for BS 5750 Part 2 could well find itself paying half the assessment fee applied to a fifty man joinery turning over £1 000 000 p.a. and heading for the same registration.

We are not privy to the assessment fees charged by the major assessing bodies but inevitably information about fees comes to us from time to time from client companies who have received quotations for assessment. Our impression is that, at 1993 rates, assessment to ISO 9002 is unlikely to cost much less than £1 000 even for the smallest company assessed by one person. Assessment to ISO 9001 would be dearer as it is more complicated.

Larger companies would be charged more, but not pro rata to the size of their payroll. Size of course is a consideration in determining assessment charges, along with other factors such as complexity of operation and intended Scope of Registration.

As well as the assessment fee, companies planning for BS 5750 should budget for the following items.

– Possible consultancy costs to help them install and activate the quality system. Even with generous grant aid this could cost the small firm at least as much as their assessment. The pros and cons of appointing a consultant are examined in the following Section 2.3.

– Possible temporary loss of business through management time devoted to development of the quality system.

– Possible additional expenses associated with BS 5750, for example, purchase of a word processor; payment of instrument calibration fees; or the cost of special training.

– Annual maintenance fees of the upkeep of the BS 5750 Certificate and the review of the quality system by an assessing body.

We stress that these figures are indicative, to provide some basis for approximate costing for small businesses who may know nothing about the subject. Firm quotations are provided to companies by assessing bodies after examination of their structure and operations and these are the only figures which count. We suggest that it is in most companies' interest to obtain quotations from two or more assessing bodies before making a decision on whether to proceed to BS 5750 but would counsel that the size of the initial assessment fee should not be the sole criterion for selection of an assessing body.

2.3   Consultancy assistance: pros and cons

Around 1990, understanding of BS 5750 in the non-engineering sector was not very advanced. Employment of a consultancy was virtually essential for most companies heading for registration. They needed specialists to help them interpret the formal language of the Standard and convert it to a practical quality system for their company. Typically the retained consultancy would help them to install their complete Documented Quality System on lines reviewed in Chapter 3. At that time, grant aided consultancy was relatively freely available through, for example, the DTI Enterprise Initiative, operated on behalf of DTI by Pera International of Melton Mowbray. Such consultancy was of generally high calibre as consultancies listed by DTI had first to satisfy demanding qualification criteria.

During the early 1990s several changes took place.

– The general awareness of BS 5750 increased.

– Many companies had acquired through business associates some understanding of the general requirements of a conforming Documented Quality System to BS 5750 before making any commitment to it.

– DTI consultancy funding became less available. A previous allocation of two grant aided consultancies was reduced to one in 1991 and it was announced that the Enterprise Initiative Scheme was scheduled for termination by 1994.

– In some areas, new consultancy funding sources opened up through quangos such as Enterprise Companies, most of which offered low cost consultancy on BS 5750 to small firms in their area. Frequently this operated on a co-operative basis, with twelve to fifteen small companies from the same industrial sector forming a 'quality club' and proceeding to BS 5750 under the tutelage of a consultancy. Selection criteria for consultants to these bodies were not always as rigorous as those imposed by the DTI and there was ineffective delivery of some consultancy projects. Nevertheless the general quality awareness of many companies was improved.

Where does this leave companies, particularly small ones, planning development to BS 5750 in the mid 1990s? We suggest the following steps.

1 Make full use of texts such as this one which seek to save you money by placing before you the basis of a conforming Documented Quality System.
2 Do your best to convert the specimen Quality Manual and procedures provided in the text to the precise needs of your company. Remember that they have to state exactly what happens in *your* organisation. Do not overclaim in any way and do not sweep anything under the carpet.
3 Once this has been completed, you should have a Documented Quality System ready to put into operation. Then, review where you stand in relation to BS 5750. Can you proceed alone from here to assessment? If you consider that you can, then you have no apparent need for consultancy assistance.
4 An excellent way of establishing your status against BS 5750 at this point is to audit your emergent quality system against the checklists provided in Appendix 3. They were devised exactly for that purpose and should soon indicate to you whether you are in control.
5 If you identify a need for consultancy at this stage, at least you have already cut costs substantially by having yourself written much of the documentation required by the Standard in your business.

6 Your brief to a consultant then reduces considerably from that of a firm commissioning consultancy services from the beginning. You may be confident enough to proceed with the consultancy on the basis of a short-term contract giving them a restricted remit, for example, to audit your status against BS 5750 and to propose remedial measures for any fault found.

7 In choosing a consultancy, look for one which has experience of your industry or, failing that, one with evidence of relevant alternative credentials, for example, work experience in a related industry. You should expect commitment from the consultancy to the Process Control and related practical aspects of your business and not simply to the documentary requirements of BS 5750.

2.4 Time taken to install, develop and implement BS 5750

This varies considerably. We now observe a tendency for firms to move faster to BS 5750 than was the case in 1990. We believe that this reflects growing awareness of BS 5750 by business and not overconfidence or underestimation by firms of the severity of assessment to BS 5750.

In 1990, a BS 5750 development programme lasting from one to two years was not uncommon. Three years later we increasingly met companies who proceeded from inception to assessment in less than six months, including writing their Documented Quality System.

We do not particularly recommend so fast a programme but if the commitment is there, there seem to us to be no valid reasons for deferring assessment unduly. Assessing bodies look for some months' evidence of an active quality system to BS 5750 when they carry out assessment to BS 5750. 'Some months' can mean as few as three or it may be five depending on the assessing body. Therefore rapid progress to BS 5750 is condoned by them provided that everything is in position and there is documented evidence of an active quality system to BS 5750 for 'some months'.

2.5 Scope of Registration to BS 5750

The Scope of Registration defines the type and range of a firm's products or services offered and the related processes which they wish to submit to assessment to BS 5750. As the Scope appears on an appendix to the Certificate of Registration to BS 5750 awarded to each qualifying firm, it is important to get it right.

It is essential to omit from your Scope any activities or products which you intend to leave outside the BS 5750 quality system. It is quite legitimate for a paint manufacturer (for example) to seek BS 5750 registration for manufacture of their paint but not their varnishes. In that case permissible wording of their Scope could be on the lines 'Manufacture and distribution of paints' whereas 'Manufacture and distribution of paints and varnishes' would clearly be unacceptable.

In that situation a firm might well ask itself why varnishes could not also be pulled into the BS 5750 system and if practicable, do so. However if it saw good reasons for omitting varnishes from the 'Scope', it would meet the requirements of the Standard by adopting the restricted Scope relating to paints only.

It is useful to identify the intended Scope at an early stage as it defines the boundaries of both the Documented Quality System and the ultimate registration.

Ideally the Scope should be as definitive as possible to avoid possible ambiguities. On the other hand we sometimes encounter firms whose proposed Scope carries a risk of restricting their commercial development by being too influenced by short-term considerations. This should be avoided.

For example take the case of a firm engaged in reclamation of engine oil by purification of used car engine oil who have opted for a Scope on the following lines: 'reclamation of engine oil by purification of used car engine oils'.

If the firm were to consider that it might extend its future intake or raw material to used marine, aeroplane or other types of oil, it would be prudent to consider a slightly more flexible Scope along the lines of: 'reclamation and supply of engine oil by purification of used engine oils'.

Some day that firm might be grateful for the simple omission of the one word 'car'. If in doubt, talk over your intended Scope with your prospective assessment body at an early stage of your drive to BS 5750 and be guided by them.

Should a firm wish to extend its Scope after registration to BS 5750, that would be a matter of negotiation with their assessing body who would readily accommodate it subject to a limited reassessment against the revised Scope

2.6 A model Action Plan for BS 5750: from inception to assessment

This plan is based on a medium scale manufacturing firm employing fifty people and wishing to progress to assessment to BS 5750 only six months after initiation of their BS 5750 drive. As this is fast progress, contact with an assessing body or bodies is recommended right at the beginning of their plan. These bodies need to plan assessments well ahead and appreciate advance notice. For simplicity we have also assumed that either the firm is capable of writing and implementing its BS 5750 system unaided or, if not, that a consultant or adviser on BS 5750 has been identified by them *before* Month 1 and is available to the firm from the outset of the programme.

The basis of the plan is that certain core elements of the Documented Quality System are identified for writing and implementation during Months 1 and 2. These are the ones which are likely to be new to a firm embarking on BS 5750 and are listed in paragraph 1.8 below. They enable important external contacts to be initiated and essential internal quality records to be completed and filed, thereby affording traceable evidence of an active quality system for the four to six months leading to assessment.

Work on realigning the firm's existing procedures for process control, packaging and inspection to BS 5750 is deferred till Months 3 to 4, on the reasoning that the firm is likely to have been in control of these areas before embarking on BS 5750. That is not to say that these procedures will necessarily transfer to BS 5750 entirely unaltered, but their conversion to documents complying with BS 5750 should be easy compared with writing those of paragraph 1.8.

The plan also relies heavily on regular auditing of the emerging quality system to BS 5750 by means of the checklists provided in Appendix 3. We have found these checklists valuable in highlighting defects and indicating the necessary corrective actions to remedy them. They depend upon auditing compliance against each clause of BS 5750 Part 2 as opposed to auditing specific areas or departments of the company.

We consider the clause audits to be more revealing than departmental audits at this early stage of proceedings. Area and departmental audits could well form part of a continuing audit programme after assessment, depending on how many areas or departments there are in the company.

Model Action plan for BS 5750: from inception to assessment

Month 1

1.1 Contact assessing body/bodies; make them aware of your plans; invite a response, including a quotation for assessment, registration and post-registration surveillance and maintenance.

1.2 Prepare the first draft of the Master Quality Manual (see Chapter 3).

1.3 Appoint a Management Representative for BS 5750 and at least one deputy.

1.4 Have them trained in Internal Quality Auditing.

1.5 Appoint a Document Controller to BS 5750.

1.6 Have him/her trained in Document Control to BS 5750.

1.7 Plan general awareness training on BS 5750 for all.

1.8 Begin to write Operating Procedures, Quality Records and Operating Instructions (see Chapter 3). Suggested priorities are those for contract control; document control; purchasing; control of test and measuring equipment; control of nonconformance; corrective action; internal quality auditing and training.

1.9 As may be required by the procedures of paragraph 1.8, make contact with third parties *now*. Send, for example, quality questionnaires to your major suppliers and subcontractors (see Chapter 8); identify an instrument calibrating company; and contact any specialist trainers you may need.

Month 2

2.1 Study the responses from the assessing bodies. Assuming you are still on course for assessment at the end of Month 6, appoint the body of your choice and arrange the assessment date(s).

2.2 Proceed with preparation of the procedures listed in paragraph 1.8. Finalise them now if possible.

2.3 Draw up your forward plan for internal quality auditing (see Chapter 6).

*2.4 Start training employees for BS 5750 and recording it *now*.

*2.5 Carry out your first internal quality audits *now*.

*2.6 Start recording all nonconformances and corrective actions *now*.

2.7 Study questionnaires returned from subcontractors and suppliers.

2.8 Based on 2.7 and historic records, begin to grade subcontractors and suppliers.

2.9 Draw up a provisional list of approved subcontractors and

suppliers.
*Action on these points in Month 2 is recommended to provide four months' evidence of an active quality system on assessment.

Month 3
By now your documented quality system (DQS) should be taking shape and should be active in many areas.

3.1 Carry out a detailed internal quality audit of your emergent documented quality system using the audit checklists of Appendix 3.

3.2 Take recorded corrective action on all deficiencies found. At this early stage there will be plenty. There will be procedures and records found to be inaccurate or not yet written. There will be others which have been written but which are not being used properly. The audit will focus attention on this and indicate the necessary remedial action to you.

3.3 Evaluate the work load of the above tasks, make the necessary provisions of time and people and *start now*.

3.4 Set deadlines for completion of the corrective actions revealed by 3.1. Give priority to finalisation and implementation of the core procedures of paragraph 1.8. Ensure that they are fully active by Month 3.

3.5 As everything *must* be accurate by the end of Month 6, set Month 5 as the completion date for all other actions revealed by the above audit.

3.6 Start work on preparation of procedures and records not covered by paragraph 1.8. These are mainly concerned with areas of your operation that will have been under control before BS 5750 (for example, process control; storage, packaging, handing and distribution; test and inspection) but will nevertheless be likely to need some amendment to BS 5750.

Month 4
Now is a good time to check whether you are still on course for assessment at the end of Month 6. If you have been seriously delayed for some reason, tell your assessing body now and request a postponement. Given such generous notice they should accommodate your revised date, or defer the decision, without any difficulty.

4.1 Review the Master Quality Manual already drafted at stage 1.2 and amend it to near compliance. You will have a further opportunity to review it for total accuracy later in the programme.

4.2 Review procedures and quality records written so far and amend them to compliance.

4.3 Continue with preparation of the remainder with the view to finalising them by the end of Month 5.

4.4 Continue to audit all 18 clauses of BS 5750 against the checklists of Appendix 3 and take necessary remedial action. Check whether you have provided for the points listed below and if not, do so by the end of Month 5.

4.4. Is your Scope of Registration as stated in your manual accurate?

4.4.2 Are the Board in full agreement with it?

4.4.3 Have you carried out a first recorded Management Review of your BS 5750 system?

4.4.4 Have you fully defined control of your contracts?

4.4.5 Is your Document Control Procedure in operation?

4.4.6 Is everyone using it correctly?

4.4.7 Have you had replies to all questionnaires sent to suppliers and subcontractors?

4.4.8 If not, have you sent reminders?

4.4.9 Have you listed your main suppliers and subcontractors?

4.4.10 Are all purchases being made in conformity with your purchasing procedure?

4.4.11 Are you handling 'purchaser supplied product' (if any) satisfactorily?

4.4.12 Are you marking your products clearly and keeping clear records to afford 'traceability' if vital in your operation?

4.4.13 Are your process control procedures and records up to date and accurate?

4.4.14 Do all employees have clear work instructions for their tasks?

4.4.15 Are all your processes in control?

4.4.16 Are your test and inspection procedures and records up to date and accurate?

4.4.17 Do they provide for inspection of raw materials, processes and finished products?

4.4.18 Is the calibration and monitoring of your test and measuring equipment under control to BS 5750?

4.4.19 Have you appointed someone who is responsible for calibration?

4.4.20 Is all relevant test equipment marked or otherwise identified to its calibration status?

4.4.21 Are you segregating nonconforming product and handling and recording it correctly?

4.4.22 Is it clear who are responsible for 'disposition' of non-conforming product after review?

4.4.23 Is appropriate, recorded corrective action being taken on all nonconformances?

4.4.24 Is product being handled, stored, packaged and delivered correctly and according to written procedures?

4.4.25 Have you a list of all quality records necessary for operation of your quality system?

4.4.26 Is it up to date and under on-going review?

4.4.27 Are these records well stored and held for a stated period?

4.4.28 Is internal quality auditing in operation?

4.4.29 Is appropriate action being taken on all points?

4.4.30 Have all relevant people been trained for BS 5750 as well as their normal duties?

4.4.31 Does every employee to Chairman level have a training record on file?

4.4.32 Does it show on their CV and allow for addition of further training?

4.4.33 If relevant, is statistical control under effective control?

Month 5

By now the core elements of the documented quality system identified in paragraph 1.8 of this Action Plan should be in compliance with BS 5750 and the people involved should be comfortable in operating them. The remaining elements, deferred to Months 3 and 4 for conversion from the company's previous style to BS 5750 format, should be nearing completion. If you are seriously off target this is about your last opportunity to request a deferral of assessment. However if you have shown full commitment to making BS 5750 work to this stage, you should be looking forward with confidence to assessment at the end of Month 6.

5.1 Review the status of all procedures and documents scheduled for completion by Month 5.

5.2 Where necessary, allocate resources to complete them this month.

5.3 Review the clause by clause audits so far conducted. Ensure that all corrective actions have been taken by the scheduled date or are on schedule for action.

5.4 Carry out audits of the remaining clauses so far unaudited.

5.5 Set appropriate deadlines for completion of nonconformances resulting from the audits. Critical nonconformances should be rectified before assessment.

Month 6

This is substantially a rerun of Month 5 with the following additions set out below.

6.1 Review the Master Quality Manual and make any final amendments to bring it to total compliance. If it has altered significantly since you provided a draft inspection copy to your assessing body at an earlier stage in proceedings, inform them of the changes. If requested, provide them with a copy of the latest issue.

6.2 Review the remainder of the Documented Quality System and plug any gaps.

6.3 Carry out a mock assessment of your operation to BS 5750, if necessary enlisting outside assistance, and act on all non-conformances found.

6.4 Carry out a second Management Review of the quality system.

6.5 Audit the general 'readiness for assessment' of your company. The checklist of Stage 4 (all 33 elements) is worth rerunning at this stage. By this stage you should be looking for the answer 'Yes' to all of them.

6.6 Arrange to provide any facilities requested by your assessing body (for example, an office and access to a telephone) for your imminent assessment.

Chapter 3

How to write a Documented Quality System (DQS) to BS 5750/ISO 9000

Contents of chapter:

3.1 Three tier and simpler Documented Quality Systems
3.2 The Master Quality Manual
3.3 Operating Procedures
3.4 Quality Records and Work Instructions
3.5 A model DQS for a typical manufacturing company
3.6 A model DQS for a typical small service company

3.1   Three tier and simpler Documented Quality Systems

The declared policy of assessing bodies to BS 5750 on Documented Quality Systems (DQS) to BS 5750 is not to dictate to companies how they should write and set out their DQS but rather to accept any clearly expressed system provided it addresses and meets all relevant requirements of the Standard. There has however been such widespread adoption of the so-called three tier DQS by industry that it is prudent to examine it in some detail here. We would go further and suggest that unless a company heading for BS 5750 registration is already irretrievably committed to an alternative system, they have nothing to lose and much to gain by adopting the three tier system or, as may be appropriate to smaller firms, its slimmer variant, the two tier system.

There are sound reasons for this.

1 All assessing bodies carry out a 'desktop' evaluation of their client companies' DQS before assessment. It is decidedly 'assessor friendly' to present it to them in a familiar, logical format, which readily enables them to assess the validity of the client's DQS and to gain an insight to the company's processing or service functions before assessment.

2 It is helpful to list your general policy statements on how you satisfy the 20 clauses of BS 5750, Part 1 or the 18 of BS 5750, Part 2 in a slim Master Quality Manual, (which is Tier 1 of the system), quite separately from Tier 2 (which are your operating procedures) and Tier 3 (your quality records and work instructions).

Small firms may combine layers 2 and 3 thereby operating a two tier system.

3 By doing so, you provide a document which gives away no company secrets but does tell a customer (and an assessor) the essential facts about your business and its organisation and outlines your system for coping responsibly with BS 5750. Tiers 2 and 3 are concerned with your own company practices and should only be made available to a third party under due confidentiality.

Thus the three tier DQS consists of the following.

Tier 1

A Master Quality Manual: a series of policy statements, generally running to only 30 or so pages in total, some of which may consist of only a few sentences stating how you meet the requirements of particular clauses of BS 5750 (see Section 3.2 for how to write a Master Quality Manual).

Tier 2

Operating Procedures: a series of procedures fleshing out the Master Manual and stating in full detail how you control all relevant areas of your operation in conformity with BS 5750 (see Section 3.3 for further details).

Tier 3

Quality Records and Operating Instructions: documents giving very precise data (see Section 3.4 for further details).

The three tier DQS is sometimes shown as a triangle, as in Figure 1, because in medium to large firms the volume of documents increases considerably as we move down from Tier 1 to Tier 3. Remember that the Master Manual may only have about 30 pages. In addition to the Master Manual, medium to large firms may have 40 or more procedures some of which may run to a number of pages. They may also have many Quality Records and Work Instructions. Thus a fairly broad based triangular shape is representative of such firms.

Small firms generally operate with appreciably less documentation so that the triangular shape of the three tier system for a typical small firm is likely to be much slimmer. They may be able to accommodate their quality records and work instructions in their operating procedures thereby slimming down to a two tier system.

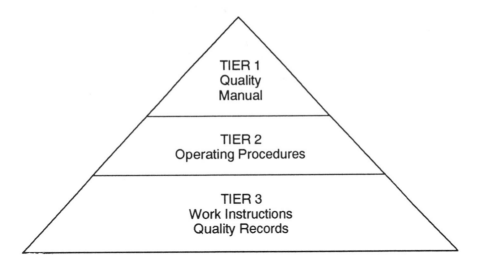

Figure 1 Three tier Documented Quality System diagram

3.2   The Master Quality Manual

The Master Quality Manual to BS 5750 Part 2 for a representative manufacturing company is given in Appendix 1. For most manufacturing and assembly firms, Part 2 of BS 5750 is appropriate. However if you are in manufacturing with an appreciable design element you should seek advice on whether BS 5750 Part 1 is more appropriate for you and, if so, adapt the manual accordingly. If you are in service rather than manufacture you should benefit from a study of Chapter 12 which should enable you to adapt the Quality Manual of Appendix 1 to reflect your service specialisation.

As you read Appendix 1, please note the following points.

1 The entire document runs to only 23 pages. Preparation of your Master Quality Manual need not therefore be a major task for you if you base it upon the example provided. Certainly it will be considerably easier than trying to write it on the basis of BS 5750: Part 2 which offers no guidance on preparation of manuals or procedures.

2 Each page is formally numbered and marked with its issue date and issue status. Companies' methods of paginating and marking documents vary considerably and if the method used in

Appendix 1 does not suit your company you should amend it to your preference.

3 Page 1 describes the company.

4 Page 2 states the company quality policy which is a mandatory requirement.

5 Page 3 indicates the distribution of the Quality Manual which is another mandatory requirement.

6 Page 4 indicates how the Quality Manual is maintained – another mandatory requirement.

7 Pages 5–23 indicate how the manufacturer addresses the requirements of the 18 clauses of BS 5750:1987, Part 2.

Some Manuals also contain an Appendix giving further information such as a summary of the operating procedures and quality records supportive of the Manual. While this is valuable information to incoming assessors it could also be useful to a rival should the Manual fall into their hands. We therefore recommend holding the Manual to a restricted format in the manner indicated in Appendix 1. It is a simple matter to supply supplementary information (such as a list of your operating procedures) to third parties on request, subject to confidentiality.

Note the reference on the title page to 'controlled' and 'uncontrolled' copies. 'Controlled' means kept active and up to date by you. 'Uncontrolled' means not kept active and up to date by you, for example, a copy given to a customer. It is prudent to have such quality documents, or excerpts from them, marked UNCONTROLLED COPY by an appropriate person such as your management representative for BS 5750 before you pass it over.

3.3   Operating Procedures

Understandably, some companies with little previous experience of documented quality assurance find it difficult to fathom what is meant by 'operating procedures', what form they should be in and how many there should be. Operating procedures are expressed in various ways, forms and lengths by companies. We offer no hard and fast rules for writing an operating procedure beyond proposing that it should be clearly written, give an accurate account of what actually happens in the area described and be formally paginated and headed.

We give below a system with which we and our clients are comfortable and which has met the requirements of assessors to date. It is based on the following simple principles, illustrated with reference to 'Part 2' of BS 5750 but equally applicable in principle to 'Part 1'.

1 There are eighteen clauses of BS 5750, Part 2, numbered 4.1 to 4.18.

2 The Master Quality Manual briefly addresses each clause as in Appendix 1.

3 We regard the undernoted clauses of BS 5750, Part 2 as 'generic' since they apply to all firms irrespective of their business and we prepare a short Operating Procedure to address each clause.

In our view, 'generic' clauses of BS 5750, Part 2 (applying to all firms in very similar format) are:

4.1   Management responsibility
4.2   Quality system
4.4   Document control
4.7   Product identification and traceability
4.12 Control of nonconforming product
4.13 Corrective action
4.15 Quality records
4.16 Internal quality audits
4.17 Training.

4 We then identify which of the undermentioned non-generic clauses of BS 5750 apply to the client firm and prepare operating procedures for them unless the statements against each in their Master Quality Manual are sufficiently definitive. Clauses from the following list which may be superfluous to some firms are 4.6 (if they do not handle product supplied by their purchaser), 4.10 (if they use no inspection, testing and measuring equipment) and 4.18 (if they use no statistical techniques). Simple statements to that effect should be made in their Master Quality Manual.

We consider the 'non generic' clauses of BS 5750, Part 2 (requiring careful adaptation to the precise requirements of individual firms) to be:

4.3   Contract review
4.5   Purchasing
4.6   Purchaser supplied product
4.8   Process control
4.9   Inspection and testing
4.10 Inspection, testing and measuring equipment
4.11 Inspection and test status
4.14 Handling, storage, packaging and delivery
4.18 Statistical techniques.

5 We believe that it clarifies a firm's documented quality system if, from the outset, operating procedures are numbered to trace to the parent clause of BS 5750. For example, Process Control pro-

cedures to BS 5750, Part 2 which are numbered 8.1, 8.2, and so on, are readily identifiable to the eighth Clause, 4.8, of the Standard. Similarly, procedures prefixed '5' would define Purchasing (Clause 4.5) and those prefixed '9' the Inspection and Testing procedures (Clause 4.9). Note the phrase 'from the outset'. It would be tedious to impose this numbering system on a DQS which already had been written. Section 3.5 provides further details.

6 We also believe that quality records relating to operating procedures benefit from similar traceability and recommend that quality records relating to a test and inspection procedure numbered 9.1 be numbered 9.1.1, 9.1.2, and so on, where practicable. Again the numbering of quality records should preferably evolve with the system and not be imposed on it once written. Again, Section 3.5 provides further details.

3.4   Quality Records and Work Instructions

This is the base of the three tier documented quality system depicted in Figure 1 in Section 3.1. Companies' requirements vary considerably here. A very small firm may be controlled by only a handful of operating instructions and quality records. A larger firm or even a small one with many processes and operations may need many more.

In our view any record filled in routinely as part of the BS 5750 quality system should be regarded as a 'Quality Record'. By this definition quality records would include (for example) management review reports, internal quality audit reports and corrective action reports as well as process control charts, inspection records and suchlike. A work instruction on the other hand conveys information to people on how to carry out their job and does not normally require entry of data by an operator followed by scrutiny by a supervisor.

Ideally all quality records and work instructions should be clearly marked with at least the date of issue, the issue number and the authority for issue but as it is sometimes difficult to afford this with externally generated documents, a practical compromise is suggested below.

Quality Records

We identify two types of quality record in our clients' operations and treat them differently as follows:

1 Quality Records which have been instituted during the writing and implementation of the Documented Quality System. These are in effect annexes of the newly written operating procedures and are therefore easy to head up and number to trace to their parent procedure as described in paragraph 6 of Section 3.3 (see the following Section 3.5 for examples).
2 Quality records which have been in satisfactory service to a firm before their BS 5750 drive and which they wish to retain substantially unaltered for some time. By their nature they may be difficult to head up in the conforming BS 5750 manner during the busy run up to assessment.

   We have so far found assessors to BS 5750 sympathetic to this classification and they have not taken a hard line on a few 'traditional' quality records allowed to continue in circulation for a period, without being formally headed to BS 5750, provided:
   a) that readily alterable records have been correctly headed
   b) that arrangements are in hand to alter remaining ones to conformity over a reasonable time scale
   c) that their purpose and issue status are evident.

Work Instructions

Again we wish to distinguish between documents generated internally and those from outside the company such as workshop manuals and machine operating instructions.

   Assessors expect to see internally generated work instructions to be headed appropriately with authority, for example, for issue or date. It is generally not too onerous to carry this out during preparation for assessment and it should certainly be done if practicable. Wall and machine mounted instructions should not be forgotten. Temporary handwritten instructions are allowable and these too should show the authority for issue and date of issue.

   We suggest that important externally generated work instructions such as workshop manuals, etc., should simply be listed in the document control procedure and issued to the people who need them (see Section 4.2 for further details).

3.5   A model DQS for a typical manufacturing company

The model used is a large dairy which conforms to the three tier system described in Section 3.1, consisting of:
1 Master Quality Manual

2 Operating Procedures
3 Quality Records/Work Instructions.
A specimen Master Quality Manual for a comparable company is given in Appendix 1. The operating procedures and quality records are given here.

Operating Procedures

These are to the system described in Section 3.3. Note that in the main, a single procedure is considered sufficient for the 'generic' clauses as previously defined but that several procedures are necessary for key 'non-generic' clauses of the company's operations such as 4.8 Process control and 4.9 Inspection and testing because of stringent food industry requirements in those areas.

Process control is defined by a comprehensive range of short procedures, each addressing the company's obligations under the Food Safety Act 1990 and related regulations. We have learned to favour this modular approach as it encourages companies to review their total process control coverage and to make suitable provisions.

As a large dairy is under consideration, with continuous pasteurisation and sterilisation of dairy products and high speed packaging, their controls are rigorous and their DQS extensive. A typical small joinery or engineering workshop could be addressed by about a third that number of procedures. They would need fewer process control procedures, perhaps only a single test and inspection procedure and would be unlikely to need procedures for Clauses 4.6 and 4.18.

A proposed list of Operating procedures to cover the dairy under consideration is given below in Table 1.

On the following page a proposed list of Quality Records for such a company is given in Table 2.

Table 1 Proposed list of Operating Procedures to BS 5750: 1987, Part 2, for a large dairy

QR Number	Purpose of Record
1.1	Management review
2.1	QA system
3.1	Contract initiation, control and review
4.1	Document control
5.1	Purchasing
5.2	Supplier and subcontractor assessment

7.1	Product identification and traceability
7.2	Product recall
8.1	GMP and Due Diligence compliance protocol
8.2	New product development
8.3	Selection and commissioning of new equipment
8.4	Plant maintenance
8.5	Plant cleaning and sanitisation
8.6	Control of personal hygiene
8.7	Product protection
8.8	Good housekeeping
8.9	Pest control
8.10	Bar code verification
8.11	Product shelf life evaluation
8.12	Control of specifications
8.13	Control of pasteurisation processes
8.14	Control of sterilisation processes
8.15	Control of product filled weights
8.16	Waste control
9.1	Inspection and testing of incoming materials
9.2	Inspection and testing of processes
9.3	Inspection and testing of finished products
9.4	Summary of test and inspection methods
10.1	Calibration and monitoring of test and measuring equipment
11.1	Marking of inspection and test status
12.1	Control of nonconforming product
12.2	Review and disposition of nonconforming product
12.3	Customer concession
13.1	Corrective action
14.1	Handling, storage, packaging and delivery
15.1	Control of quality records
16.1	Internal quality auditing
17.1	Training
18.1	Statistical process control
18.2	Sampling

Table 2 Proposed list of typical Quality Records for a large dairy. Their relationship with the list of operating procedures of Table 1 is clear by virtue of the point numbering system.

QR Number	Purpose of Record
1.1.1	Management review record
4.1.1	Document change request note
5.1.1	List of approved suppliers
5.2.1	Subcontractor assessment record
7.2.1	Product recall/reconciliation record
8.2.1	New product development record
8.3.1	Plant commissioning record
8.4.1	Plant maintenance record
8.5.1	Plant cleaning/sanitisation record
8.6.1	Personal hygiene record
8.7.1	Product protection record
8.9.1	Pest control record
8.10.1	Bar code verifier
8.11.1	Product shelf life record
8.13.1	Pasteurisation efficiency record(s)
8.14.1	Sterilisation efficiency record(s)
8.15.1	Product filled weight records
9.1.1 to 9.1.4	Test and inspection records
10.1.1	List of approved calibration subcontractors
10.1.2	Instrument verification record
12.1.1	Nonconformance report
12.1.2	Disposition record for nonconforming product
12.1.3	Concession request form
13.1.1	Corrective action report
14.1.1	Packaging integrity record
16.1.1	Quality audit report
16.1.2	Quality audit nonconformance report
17.1.1	Employee CV, induction and initial training record
17.1.2	Employee continuing training record

3.6   A model DQS for a typical small service company

Again this is similar to the three tier system described in Section 3.1. The DQS is that of our own practice, MPA, consulting industrial chemists. The Master Quality Manual for MPA's system follows the format of that of the manufacturer given in Appendix 1 but the resemblance ends there. Our system is under development to BS 5750, Part 1 and we address each of its twenty clauses in terms of service and not manufacture.

Note how different our lists of procedures and quality records are compared with those of a manufacturer. We are involved with product and process design for some clients and this is reflected in the presence of three design procedures. We were able to define and control our operation with only 12 operating procedures compared with the 40 for the large dairy reviewed in Section 3.5. We considered that sufficiently definitive statements had already been made in our Quality Manual on those clauses of the Standard not made the subject of operating procedures.

The operating procedures are however backed with 29 quality records and work instructions as listed in Table 4

We believe that MPA's twelve operating procedures of only about four pages each on average is towards a minimum for BS 5750 whereas the 40 of the large dairy is towards the top end of the scale.

Table 3 Operating Procedures to control the small consultancy MPA to BS 5750, Part 1

QR Number	Purpose of Record
1.1	Management review
3.1	Contract control and review
4.1	Design of consultancy projects
4.2	Design of new products
4.3	Design of new plant
5.1	Document control
9.1	Control of processes (consultancy projects)
13.1	Control of nonconformances
14.1	Corrective action
17.1	Internal quality auditing
17.2	Auditing of clients' operations
18.1	Recruitment and training

Table 4 Quality Records and Work Instructions to control the consultancy MPA to BS 5750, Part 1

QR Number	Purpose of Record
1.1.1	Quality system review by management
3.1.1	Contract planner, ad hoc projects
3.1.2	Contract planner, formal contracts
4.1.1	Consultancy design planner
4.1.2	New product design planner and record
4.1.3	New plant design planner and record
5.1.1	Document change request
5.1.2	Record of all controlled documents
5.1.3	Summary of document review procedure
5.1.4	Summary of archive storage
6.1.1	Register of approved subcontractors
9.1.1	Client visit report as Qualified Person (QP)
9.1.2	Client visit planner and report not as Qualified Person
9.1.3	Consultancy work record
9.1.4	Client visit planner: GMP compliance audits on food factories
9.1.5	Client visit planner on behalf of principals
10.1.1	Client report on MPA's project efficiency
10.1.2	Document pre-release cross check routine
10.1.3	MPA's house rules
10.1.4	Pre-travel document and equipment checklist
11.1.1	Instrument verification protocol
13.1.1	Service nonconformance report
13.1.2	Request for a client concession
14.1.1	Corrective action report
16.1.1	List of quality records controlling MPA
17.1.1	Internal quality audit report
17.1.2	Internal quality audit noncompliance report
17.2.1	Record of client quality audits to BS 5750 by MPA
18.1.1	Training log for MPA's staff
18.1.2	Recruitment record for subcontract consultants

Document control

Contents of chapter:

4.1   How to identify, mark and control your documents

As a well organised Documented Quality System is essential to BS 5750, it follows that all documents forming part of the quality system need to be under tight control. BS 5750 requires quality documents to be subject to the following controls:

a) revision and approval for issue by authorised people

b) availability of current issues of documents at all relevant locations

c) prompt removal of all obsolete documents from all locations

d) revision and approval of document changes by authorised people (generally the original approvers)

e) the indication of the nature of any document change in the document if practicable

f) the drawing up of a master list to show identify the current, approved issue of each document

g) the reissue of documents after a practical number of changes have been made

h) the retention period of quality records stated.

An example of a conforming Document Control Procedure for a representative company, embodying the above requirements of the Standard, is given in the following Section 4.2. The procedure is to a format with which we are comfortable but it is no more than one example of a conforming procedure, for adaptation as may be wished. In this instance (only) the full procedure is given on pages 39 to 44. Further procedures provided in this text are given in abridged form for adaptation to the format of the document control procedure or an alternative preferred form.

For your guidance, those parts of the procedure which meet

each of these requirements and have been marked with an asterisk and the relevant prefix letter from the above list, for example, * a); * b), and so on.

It goes without saying that the asterisks and letters would not carry over into a 'live' procedure. They are only there, for the purposes of this text, to indicate that all relevant controls have been incorporated into the procedure.

4.2   A model Document Control Procedure to BS 5750

Note 1 The procedure is numbered 4.1 to trace to Clause 4.1 of BS 5750, Part 2 (5.1 would be appropriate for BS 5750, Part 1).
Note 2 In this instance all pages of the procedure are given in pages 39 to 44 inclusive.

**STANDARD OPERATING PROCEDURE
No: 4.1: DOCUMENT CONTROL**

Issue number: **First**   Date of issue: **1.1.93**

Number of pages in this document: One plus three appendices

Originated by: Quality Manager

Approved by: Deputy Quality Manager*(a)

Amendments made to this procedure: See page (i) *(e)

Contents

Basis of document control procedure   p 1

Appendix 1: Document change form   p 2 *(d)

Appendix 2: List of approved documents with distribution
                    list of holders   p 3 *(b)

Appendix 3: Review procedure for approved documents   p 4 *(d)

Circulation of the document

Please list all holders of this procedure here:

Model Document Control Procedure, cont'd:

LIST OF AUTHORISED AMENDMENTS TO PROCEDURE 4.1

Eight amendments are allowed, after which the procedure is withdrawn and formally reissued. Details of all amendments are entered to the table below *(e) and *(f).

Paragraph amended	Details of amendments	Authorised by	Approved by	Date

Model Document Control Procedure, cont'd:

Page 1 of Page 1

Issue number of page: **First**   Date of issue: **1.1.93**

Date of reissue: N/A   For reason for reissue see page (i)

1 DOCUMENT CONTROL: RESPONSIBILITIES AND PROCEDURES

1.1 All controlled documents issued by the company (as listed below) are subject to approval by the company's Document Review Panel (para 1.7) before issue/reissue through an acting Document Controller (DC) *(a).

Quality Manual   Standard Operating Procedures
Quality Records   Specifications

1.2 Active documents must only be changed in accordance with the document change procedure described in this note *(d).

1.3 A record of all controlled documents is maintained by the DC and shows:

- reference number
- issue number
- date of issue
- and, where relevant, originator(s)
- distribution *(b).

1.4 All copies of documents made obsolete by approved reissue are promptly withdrawn from distribution by the DC who visits each authorised holder and makes the necessary replacements. A single copy, marked 'withdrawn' is held by the DC on file for reference *(c).

1.5 Anyone in the company may raise a request for a document change.

1.6 A description of any proposed documentary change is entered by the proposer on a Document Change Request Note (Appendix 1, QR 4.1.1) and passed to the DC.

1.7 The originator is then invited to present his/her reasons for the proposed change to a panel comprising at least one Director and the Quality Manager.

1.8 If the change is approved, the note is initialled by the panel. *(d) The DC then withdraws the redundant document(s) and issues their replacements as in para 1.4 *(c).

1.9 The issue number and revision status of all affected pages of the relevant document are altered to reflect the change made *(b) and *(e).

Model Document Control Procedure, cont'd:

Quality Record No. **4.1.1**   Retention period: **Five years** (* h)

Title: **DOCUMENT CHANGE REQUEST RECORD**

Originator: _____   Verified by: _____

Date of issue: _____   Issue number: _____

If a reissue, reason for reissue: _____

Person issuing request: _____

Date: _____

Description of proposed change: _____

_____

Reason for proposed change: _____

_____

Evaluation of proposed change: _____

_____

Proposed change upheld?   *YES/NO* _____

Delete as appropriate. Review panel please initial and date.

Document affected by the change: _____

Change effective from: _____

Model Document Control Procedure, cont'd:

Quality Record No. **4.1.2**   Retention period: **Indefinite**

Title: **RECORD OF CONTROLLED QUALITY DOCUMENTS
          WITH HOLDERS**

Originator: _____   Verified by: _____

Date of issue: _____   Issue number: _____

If a reissue, reason for reissue: _____

Authority for issue/ reissue: _____

Document   Issue date/status   Authorised holders:

Master Quality
Manual

Operating
Procedures
(please list)

Quality Records
(please list)

Specifications
(please list)

Model Document Control Procedure, cont'd:

Quality Record No. **4.1.3**   Retention period: **Indefinite**

Title: **DOCUMENT REVIEW PROCEDURE**

Originator: _____

Date of issue: _____   Issue number: _____

If a reissue, reason for reissue: _____

Authority for issue/ reissue: _____

Please state your system for reviewing the documents controlling
quality in your business, not forgetting the review of official, 'uncontrolled' documents such as British Standard Specifications, Codes of
Practice, Regulations and so on. You might consider the use of a
commercial updating service for the latter or get yourselves on the
relevant mailing lists. For review of your internal, 'controlled' documents, employ any system you are comfortable with; for example, it
could be pulled into the Management Review twice a year.

(End of model document control procedure)

4.3   The Document Controller

Especially in its formative stages, but also after registration, control of documents to BS 5750 can be a formidable task. Large companies may need to appoint a virtually full-time Document Controller (DC) to cope with the organised issue, retrieval and reissue of the many elements of the Documented Quality System. The smallest companies obviously cannot think in those terms and must make do with available resources. For sole traders 'available resources' means you!

Companies will find their own solution according to the volume of documentation they handle and their available resources.

The very smallest companies (sole traders), who fulfil the DC role themselves, at least have the benefit of having the entire quality system under their personal control. After the initial task of writing and activating the documented quality system they also have the consolation that the maintenance of the quality system is less onerous than that of a larger company by requiring no internal circulation of documents. Sole traders are advised to make arrangements to have themselves externally audited at intervals, a subject we return to in Chapter 6. They might also have to look to external assistance if they find document upkeep too onerous.

The largest companies are probably best situated to handle the DC role if only by virtue of the magnitude of the task which cannot normally be fitted into the routine of an already appointed secretary. A new appointment (of a DC) is frequently the solution.

We find that the DC issue is most difficult to solve efficiently and cost effectively in small to medium companies of 10 to 200 employees. At the bottom end of that scale, either the Management Representative for BS 5750, or Deputy, generally fit document control into their normal duties. Much beyond twenty employees, document control begins to become an unwelcome burden on these two people and a case for secretarial assistance begins to develop. With the economic pressures on small to medium companies, pleas for a specialist DC for BS 5750 tend to fall on deaf ears. A common compromise is to train a typist to handle the job along with other duties. Although not an ideal solution, it can be made to operate effectively, and is an excellent form of management training for a typist with ambition.

Whichever route is chosen, it is imperative that the DC operates under the control of the Management Representative for BS 5750 or Deputy who typically are the people responsible for originating and formally re-originating all quality documents.

The qualifications of a good DC are a good command of English, typing ability, enthusiasm for the job, attention to detail and, preferably, ability to operate a word processor. He/she should be trained in documentation to BS 5750, either formally through an offsite short course, or internally under a trained colleague such as the Management Representative for BS 5750.

4.4   Word processor or typewriter?

The word processor (WP) might have been invented for BS 5750. As almost everyone will by now be aware, the WP is like a typewriter in having a standard QWERTY keyboard, by means of which words are typed in, exactly as with a conventional typewriter. The enormous advantages of the WP over a typewriter are that the typed text is displayed on a screen; that textual errors are readily correctable while the script is displayed on the screen; that, at the touch of a button, the WP will automatically type the script to a sheet on an annexed printer; that, at the touch of another button, the text is saved to memory, that is, held on disk available for recall and amendment as required. This means that the whole of a company's Documented Quality System to BS 5750 can be held on a couple of disks plus the same number of reserve back-up copies There are further advantages which need not be gone into here.

The use of a word processor for BS 5750 documentation is strongly recommended. If this is a point which it may seem unnecessary to labour a full decade after the widespread adoption of word processors, we still encounter small, busy firms to whom this is news. They may also harbour a fear that the WP is very expensive, very 'technical' and needs high expertise in its operation.

We seek to persuade them that small second-hand word processors with printers come on the market every week at the cost of one week's salary for an efficient typist and that the skills to operate one can be acquired in an afternoon.

It is possible to control BS 5750 documentation by means of a typewriter but as virtually each reissue would require a major if not a complete re-type, the case for installing a word processor in even the smallest company is irresistible if they are heading for BS 5750.

Part 3 – How to Consolidate BS 5750/ISO 9000

Training for BS 5750/ISO 9000

Contents of chapter:

5.1 Basic requirements to meet BS 5750
5.2 Beyond the basics
5.3 A model Training Procedure to BS 5750

5.1 Basic requirements to meet BS 5750

BS 5750 obliges us to be systematic about training by not merely carrying out quality-related training but also by recording it. In our view it is prudent to interpret 'quality-related' as applying to virtually all activities in a firm. As a minimum there should be two records summarising the training of everybody in the business:
– one giving their CV and general background
– one listing their quality-related training, both in-house and external.

There should also be a statement defining how training is to be operated and controlled by the company and how the future 'quality training' needs of employees are identified.

The proposed training records should apply to everyone in the firm from the youngest entrant to the chairman and should be updated to record additional training skills as they are acquired. Certificates (or copies) received by trainees on successful termination of training should be attached to their records.

In small to medium scale companies the role of training officer can either be assigned to an existing member of staff on an intermittent basis, or each section manager or supervisor can be made responsible for preparing and maintaining training records for those under his control. Initially a sizeable task, it soon settles down to holding a file for everyone in the particular area of control and updating it whenever an employee acquires a further training skill.

Quality related training for BS 5750 takes two forms:
– training to enable employees to carry out their designated tasks effectively in accordance with procedures
– training to give them an appreciation of BS 5750.

Awareness training for BS 5750 should be practical and free of jargon and related to the aptitude of trainees and their intended degree of involvement in the operation of the BS 5750 quality system. There is little point in exposing hourly paid operatives to the fine detail of BS 5750 and its specialised terminology but they will certainly benefit from an understanding of its general objectives, particularly as they relate to the performance and recording of their own jobs.

Awareness training for supervisors and managers can be more formalised through study, seminars, video sessions and by working along with consultants, calibration engineers and so on who may be retained to serve the company.

An outline training programme for BS 5750 awareness, structured to the requirements of all levels in a typical medium to large company might take the form noted below. This should be trimmed or adjusted as appropriate for small firms.

1   Board members, managers and supervisors

1.1 An initial awareness seminar occupying at least a morning is worth considering for all board members, managers and supervisors. Like training for internal quality auditing (Chapter 6), seminars on BS 5750 are particularly beneficial if the material is brought to life by being directed to the company's own processes and services.

Prolonged lecturing by the leaders should be avoided. As a general guide, uninterrupted lecturing on so formal a system as BS 5750 for more than fifteen minutes at a time is an error and should be resisted. Instead, the seminars should be 'interactive', with the trainees invited at intervals to divide into small groups to tackle syndicate tasks related to the topic just reviewed by the seminar leader(s).

Syndicate tasks for an awareness seminar on BS 5750 which we have found to be effective are given in Appendix 2 along with a typical seminar programme.

1.2 Training for aspects of BS 5750 for which certain managers will hold special responsibility should also be provided. This includes:
– training for document control to BS 5750. Probably this is only essential for your intended document controller (see Chapter 4 for further details).
– training for internal quality auditing to BS 5750. This may be necessary for several people depending on the size of the firm (see Chapter 6 for further details).
– training for calibration of instruments to BS 5750. This may be useful for one or more plant engineers in large firms with sophisticated instruments and test equipment having particularly demand-

ing calibration and monitoring requirements (see Chapter 9.3 for further details).

1.3 Practical 'on job' training on the application of BS 5750 to trainees' own jobs should not be overlooked as it is the most vital element of the programme. Much of it can be initiated around Month 2 on a 6 month action plan. For example purchasing staff should be trained in grading the efficiency of the company's suppliers and keeping them under review; process supervisors in monitoring their process controls and quality records; store supervisors in ensuring that goods are used in rotation and are clearly marked with essential identifiers; stock controllers and quality assurance staff in controlling the segregation, identification and 'disposition' of nonconforming stock.

For consolidating this form of training we have found the operating procedures written during preparation of the BS 5750 quality system valuable. A well written, concise operating procedure should be an excellent training aid in detailing exactly what happens in the area or function it addresses. It may have to be supplemented by more detailed departmental instructions (for example, for operation of plant) but as an initial guide to a department or section it has much to recommend it. As these procedures normally take some time to 'bed in' after introduction, their application to training may have to be deferred to about three quarters way through the action plan.

2   Line operatives

Line operatives must be effectively trained for their BS 5750-related duties as their contribution is critical to the success of the project. In principle their training requirements are similar to those of management by requiring initial awareness training for any special responsibilities for BS 5750 they may hold; and practical on-the-job training. The more practically oriented this training can be made, the better.

Initial awareness of BS 5750 can be imparted less formally and more quickly than by the seminar suggested for management. Individual firms have their own approaches to this, for example:

– informal discussions with their supervisors in small groups, or
– handouts giving the essential outline of BS 5750.

Generally, special responsibilities for BS 5750 such as document control and internal quality auditing are allocated at management/supervisor level at the outset of BS 5750 projects but there is no reason why effective quality auditors (for example) cannot be from the shop floor. If so, they should receive the same training as their more senior colleagues.

Practical 'on job' training is vital and should be reinforced during preparation for BS 5750 with special reference to additional controls and records and standards of workmanship imposed by the Standard. A summary of all such training should be entered to individuals' training logs.

5.2   Beyond the basics

Section 5.1 indicated the basic training requirements for BS 5750. This section looks beyond the basics by examining alternative training methods that might form part of the more elaborate programme of a company wishing to afford more comprehensive training.

5.2.1   College education

'Quality' has been taken on to the syllabus of many colleges in recent years. Courses vary in mode of attendance and include evening attendance; day release; block release; distance learning; and full time attendance.

In ascending order of course length and rigour, colleges provide courses as listed below. As the position alters from year to year, this is only a rough guide to indicate general possibilities. Details should be confirmed through local colleges or departments of further education.

– Short courses on BS 5750. Typically these occupy six to eight evenings and afford a useful introduction to the subject. Successful trainees may be 'certificated'. These courses are useful for people wanting specific BS 5750 knowledge without the distractions of other quality systems and techniques.

– Longer evening or day release courses leading to nationally accredited qualifications at technician level, for example, City and Guilds of London, Part 1 and Part 2 Certificates in Quality Assurance; Vocational and Educational Council Certificates for various quality-related modules. These are highly recommended but it should be noted that they may well include material outside the immediate scope of a typical BS 5750 drive. City and Guilds, Part 2, for example, deals with statistical quality control quite rigorously.

– Post graduate courses on quality assurance for students whose primary qualification may be a BSc. in science or computing (for example) although less formal entry qualifications are generally acceptable if backed by appropriate experience. Such courses frequently entail day release attendance for a year leading to a Diploma in Quality Assurance or Management and some offer a second year of more advanced studies leading to a Master's degree such as MSc. By their advanced nature these courses go well beyond BS 5750. The early graduates from these quite recently established courses speak highly of them.

5.2.2   Videos

Videos on BS 5750 have been prepared by several agencies and can serve a useful purpose at the awareness stage by affording valid training that can be entered onto a trainee's log. They are more suitable for management than for practical line operatives as they consist of a clause by clause explanation of the Standard in the form of question and answer session between a trainee and several specialists in BS 5750 .

Given the wide availability of camcorders nowadays, there is an opportunity for companies who wish to go beyond the basics of BS 5750 training to prepared house videos which depict their own situations, problems and solutions. Such videos can be very effective training aids and, of course, the audience has the thrill of recognition as a bonus.

5.2.3   Short sentence and multiple choice tests

We have never found BS 5750 particularly easy to express in terms of simple sentence construction and multiple choice tests that might form part of a more extended training programme to BS 5750. Partly this is because the Standard has been written to embrace all industrial and commercial activities and is therefore 'general' in tone. Also the borderline between conformance and nonconformance is not always clear cut in situations in industrial and commercial practice.

With perseverance we managed to prepare a few multiple choice papers for companies which are based very much on their own situations. During these exercises we formed the strong impression that, as with the videos, relating the training to the company's own processes is essential to its success. We offer the following guidelines to people wishing to progress along the same path by preparing a small bank of multiple choice questions to test their employees' general awareness of BS 5750 in their company.

1 Base all the questions on your own activities.
2 Keep them simple. You are not trying to trip people up. You are reinforcing their knowledge of quite a demanding quality system with which you are probably more familiar than the trainees as you are setting the questions.
3 Make them as 'visual' as possible. A photograph of one of your reaction vessels or an actual sample of one of your purchasing forms or products is more interesting than a sentence describing them.
4 Give people plenty of time to read and understand the paper before tackling it.
5 Discuss their paper with them on completion. Explain their errors and arrange to give them a rerun of the same paper in a few days time. You will be surprised at their improved performance the second time round.
6 Try to make your questions as clear and unambiguous as possible. This is not as easy for BS 5750 as it sounds. You may well find that some 'wrong' responses from trainees are the result of the question being unsound in some way.
7 Do not worry if your questions straddle every aspect of the company as opposed to being related to specific departments because:
   a) you will probably find it difficult to prepare a bank of meaningful multiple choice questions for every department
   b) BS 5750 is meant to encourage teamwork and company knowledge. If a purchasing assistant fails a process question first time around, he is unlikely to do so the second time and he will have increased his knowledge of the company in the process.
8 Consider constructing your questions so that they can be preceded by an opening statement such as: 'The situation shown below could fail BS 5750 because . . .'. In this way we remind ourselves to keep the question simple and related to BS 5750 assessment.
9 Then complete the question by providing one genuine response and two or three 'distractors', that are apparently believable but actually wrong responses.
10 Do not forget to vary the order in which the correct response appears from question to question.
11 As not everyone may have sat a multiple choice test before, make sure that they know what to do, for example, whether to tick or ring their preferred response; or what to do if they wish to alter their choice.
12 If you find that the multiple choice format is too restrictive, consider making some of the questions short sentence

completion or similar in type.

A number of multiple choice questions to test awareness of BS 5750 are provided in Appendix 5 to indicate general lines of approach.

5.2.4   Books and articles

Books on quality assurance form an important part of the learning processes of students on the more advanced courses described under College education in paragraph 5.2.1. There is a wide range of books on the management of quality assurance, many written by quality assurance specialists of international reputation and there are many excellent texts on the more technical aspects of quality assurance such as mathematically based sampling and inspection schemes.

Some, especially those concerned with the management aspects, are interesting reading for practising industrial and commercial managers. Of particular benefit to managers whose immediate concern is to install and implement BS 5750 in their companies and then maybe progress to Total Quality Management (TQM), are those which either specialise in the BS 5750 series or in BS 5750 linking to TQM. It is doubtful whether books of this type are particularly effective below manager/supervisor level as they are not always written in the simplest language.

Books concerned with the technical aspects of quality assurance are not particularly suitable for general managers as they are written primarily for quality specialists involved on a routine basis in application of sampling and inspection schemes of some complexity.

Papers on BS 5750 written for technical journals are generally very readable and well informed and can be an excellent way of introducing people painlessly to the subject. Much the same can be said of newspaper articles on the subject although they may not always cover the subject in sufficient depth. The fact that papers and newspaper articles may be populist in appeal is in no way to their detriment. Many a good message comes across in simple language and BS 5750 particularly benefits from a simplifying treatment. We feel that such papers and articles could form a more important part of employee awareness training for BS 5750 than at present, as they are generally well thought out, concise, clear, free and of recent origin.

5.2.5   Quality Clubs

Quality forums and clubs have been formed in recent years in which delegates from firms in the area meet to discuss matters of common quality interest. Normally their meetings are held in evenings to avoid interfering with work. Papers on quality are presented and discussed at these meetings and special events such as seminars and works visits also feature on typical forum programmes.

The quality forum represents yet another way of disseminating (and receiving) quality information. It may be to a firm's advantage to have a member or two of staff enrolled in their local forum to keep in touch with developments in quality system development.

5.3   A model Training Procedure to BS 5750

The outline of a training procedure to BS 5750 is given in the following pages. It is assumed to be for a company requiring a reasonable degree of mechanical aptitude of its employees, but no formal expertise such as tradesman status. The assumption is also made that the company has asked one of its officers to 'double up' as Training Officer. The procedure is not formatted to BS 5750. For details of formatting, see Chapter 4.

Outline operational procedure for training

Contents
Responsibilities for training
Recruitment/induction
External and internal training
Appendix 1 QR 17.1.1: Employee CV
Appendix 2 QR 17.1.2: Employee training record

Responsibilities for training
The Training Officer is responsible for training in the company. Through his training programme he will keep in touch with training courses and seminars and advise colleagues as necessary. Equally, managers and staff are encouraged to suggest suitable training as they become aware of it.

Training records are issued and collected by the Training Officer who also makes arrangements with the managers to carry out or have training carried out, internally or externally.

Each Section Manager is authorised to nominate an Instructor for the area(s) under his/her control and thus ensure that there is a means of training everyone in the business to the levels necessary for their tasks.

Each Section Manager is responsible for ensuring that on a regular basis training carried out and necessary training are recorded on the training record QR 17.1.2 for each employee in his/her control.

The Training Officer is responsible, through the Management Review Panel, for reviewing the company training policy and system.

The Training Officer has responsibilities beyond training and is a 'facilitator' of training rather than a specialist trainer.

Recruitment/induction

Evidence of appropriate technical and professional credentials is required of all applicants for positions in the following areas of the company's operations. (Please list appropriate areas e.g. laboratory; data processing; accounts.)

Recruits to hourly paid production posts are selected on the basis of neat and hygienic appearance and deportment, appropriate experience (preferably in a related industry) and evidence of reasonable mechanical and manual aptitude.

All new recruits have an introductory meeting with the Training Officer or designate who explains the company operating methods. During week 1 the recruit's aptitudes are assessed and he/she is placed in a suitable work area for detailed on the job training.

New recruits engaged on a permanent basis are trained in appropriate skills according to their placement in the company. Appropriate skills include:

Area: Office

Telephone skills; photocopying; order processing; keyboard and word processor skills; basic accounting etc.

All permanent employees are annually reviewed for the suitability and effectiveness of the in-company training they have received. Depending on the review, company training methods may be strengthened and/or employees may be directed to more suitable tasks.

Training is arranged whenever appropriate to the company's needs.

Example of training record:

Quality Record No. **17.1.1**   Retention period: **Indefinite**

Title: **EMPLOYEE CV**

Originator: (Please state) _____

Date of issue: **1.1.93**   Issue number: **1**

If a reissue, reason for reissue: **N/A** _____

Authority for issue/reissue: _____

Aim: To record the CV of   Employee
employees and indicate their
suitability for employment in their   _____
role.
Format: Details are entered to the   Date of employment
employee's personal log as below
by his/her immediate supervisor.   _____

                                          Initial appointment

                                          _____

CV: Attach copy of CV if available. If no CV available, give brief
summary of employee's background and its relation to his/her initial
placement in the company. For details of this employee's further
progress see QR 17.1.2.

Signed _____ **Date** _____
Position in company _____

Example of training record:

Quality Record No. **17.1.2**   Retention period: **Indefinite**

Title: **EMPLOYEE TRAINING RECORD**

Originator: (Please state)

Date of issue: **1.1.93**   Issue number: **1**

If a reissue, reason for reissue: **N/A**

Authority for issue/ reissue:

Aim: To record all quality-related   Employee
training received by permanently
engaged personnel from induction,   _____
through in-company training, to spe-   Date of employment
cialised 'one off' training courses.
Format: Details are entered to the   _____
employee's personal log as below by   Initial employment
his/her immediate supervisor.
                                         _____

Training received   Course details   Location/tutor Date(s) Training
                     (give full details)   review

Further details of employee's progress, e.g. promotions, diplomas etc.

Further training needs identified at the latest training review:

Date of review:

Training need identified:

Signed _____   **Date** _____

Position in company _____

Internal Quality Auditing: how to make it work for you

Contents of chapter:

6.1 Introduction to Internal Quality Auditing – aims; types; planning audits

Aims of auditing

Quality auditing originated in the USA around World War 2 as large corporations such as defence organisations needed to be sure that their quality standards and policies were being upheld both by their suppliers and by their own staff. They are now an integral part of most quality management systems and management quality standards such as BS 5750 demand them.

A dictionary definition of auditing is 'a systematic investigation or appraisal of procedures and operations to determine conformity with prescribed procedures'. This definition was originally intended to refer to financial auditing which has been in operation much longer than quality auditing but it describes quality auditing equally well.

BS 4778: Part 1, 1987 more formally describes a quality audit as 'a systematic and independent examination to determine whether quality activities and related results comply with planned arrangements and whether these arrangements are implemented effectively and are suitable to achieve objectives'. Key words and phrases in this definition illustrated with reference to a BS 5750 system are as follows.

Systematic audit
There must be a system such as the model Internal Quality Audit-

ing Procedure given in Section 6.3 to set out the objectives of the audits and the methods for conducting and recording audits.

Independent audit
The person(s) carrying out the audit ,the 'auditor(s), should be independent of the person(s) or function being audited ,the 'auditee(s). (This presents obvious difficulties for sole traders who might have to seek outside assistance to meet the 'independence' requirement of audits applied to their operations.)

Planned arrangements
The procedures which define how clauses of BS 5750 are met and the quality records which support them.

Implemented effectively
The auditee must be seen to be carrying out operations as laid down in procedures. For example, if in a procedure it is stated that 'a sample is drawn every hour, measured for length against a gauge, with the result recorded on a record', that exact procedure must be seen to take place during an audit of the process.

Quality audits may be applied, for example, to processable raw materials, to processes or services, to products, to the environment or to organisations/systems such as a BS 5750 Quality System. Readers from the healthcare, electronics, pharmaceutics and food industries will be familiar with audits of their factories and processes by regulatory inspectors and by major customers. They may also be used to applying similar audits to their suppliers and sub-contractors. Such audits may have a somewhat different intent from audits to assess compliance with BS 5750, by concentrating on Due Diligence, Good Manufacturing Practice and on hygienic and safe manufacture. This chapter addresses internal quality auditing to BS 5750. Internal quality audits are those carried out by a company on its own practices and are the 'first party audits' described in the next section.

Quality auditing is a sampling process whereby selected aspects of a process or system are examined. By its nature it cannot therefore cover the A to Z of a department or function (which would be cumbersome and time consuming). It is similar in principle to the 'activity sampling' practised by work study engineers by relying on a series of short observations of activities or procedures to a pre–planned programme. Deficiencies are noted, drawn to the attention of the 'auditees' and corrected. A successful departmental audit cannot therefore be a total bill of quality health, nor is it intended to be. Its usefulness lies more in its ability to highlight deficiencies which might have continued uncorrected but for the audit.

Types of audit

There are many definitions of audit types. Three of particular significance to companies progressing to BS 5750 are as follows.

1 First Party Audits such as internal quality audits. These are conducted by a company on its own procedures and are an essential component of their BS 5750 compliance programme. Failure to conduct them properly will almost certainly result in failure of assessment to BS 5750. A model procedure for 'internal quality auditing' in the BS 5750 mode is given in Section 6.3. As it differs in some important details from other auditing procedures. It is worthy of study and adaptation to individual companies' requirements.

2 Second Party Audits. These are audits carried out on a firm by 'second parties' such as its customers and may or may not be concerned with BS 5750 compliance. It is incidentally beneficial for a firm to have a second party audit to BS 5750 carried out itself before its official 'Third Party Audit' to BS 5750, as indication of necessary corrective actions will help improve its quality system and therefore its readiness for assessment. Some companies carry out second party audits of their suppliers but as this is not a mandatory requirement of the 1987 versions of BS 5750, we will concentrate on planning and operation of the mandatory first party audits in this chapter.

3 Third Party Audits. These are audits carried out on a firm by an official assessing body to examine compliance against a defined standard such as the *Medicines Act, The Food Safety Act, The Environmental Protection Act* or of immediate relevance to this chapter, to BS 5750. Assessment to BS 5750 by an assessing body is a comprehensive Third Party Audit.

Before an assessing body may carry out Third Party Audits to BS 5750 it must first be certified by the overseeing body NACCB (National Accreditation Council for Certifying Bodies). There are currently twenty five accredited assessing bodies to BS 5750 in the UK, the most prominent of which is BSiQA, which has a chain of regional offices in the UK and several abroad, including one in Washington DC, USA.

Planning internal quality audits

There are normally five elements in the planning of internal quality audits.

1 The audit schedule

This is a plan of forthcoming audits, indicating the sections or functions to be audited, with the times and dates of the audits and is made available to relevant people before it is put into operation. A basic version of such a plan is given in the Internal Quality Auditing Procedure in Section 6.3. Once the quality system has been installed, a monthly frequency of auditing is fairly typical but in the period leading to assessment it is recommended that a higher frequency of auditing be applied. The general aims of pre–assessment audits should be to verify that the clauses of BS 5750 have been correctly addressed and provided for in the newly created Documented Quality System and that the firm complies with them.

2 Notifying the auditees

An audit to BS 5750 should never be a snap inspection. Auditees should be given reasonable notice of audits to be carried out on their area of control. This enables them to prepare the necessary information, to allocate staff to take the auditors around the plant as necessary and generally to tidy up before the audit. This is not as artificial a situation as may appear at first sight. Despite being given generous advance warning, a department which is struggling and seriously adrift of compliance with BS 5750 is unlikely to receive a clean bill of health from the audit team.

3 Obtaining and reviewing the documentation

The audit team should be provided beforehand with the procedures, specifications, work instructions and quality records used to control the area to be audited. They should also be provided with any other relevant documents they may ask for in advance, such as records of previous audits and inspections and the area's corrective action file.

4 Preparing an audit checklist

Based on the above information, a checklist should be prepared covering all aspects to be pulled into the scope of the audit. The checklists provided in Appendix 3 indicate one way of approaching their preparation. Each list is a series of questions which focus thought by demanding a straight answer – generally *Yes* or *No*. It should be noted that these checklists were devised to audit a firm's status against each clause of BS 5750 during the emergent phase of its Documented Quality System. They have been found useful for that purpose. In some situations, particularly small companies with few departments and a limited range of processes or services, we have also found them useful after registration to BS 5750. We advise that they be adapted to individual requirements and reviewed and varied at intervals, otherwise the audits could become too predictable.

In Appendix 4 examples have been provided of process control checklists which are more detailed than the general ones of Appendix 3 by asking very specific questions for key processing aspects of a food processor's operations. These are particularly useful to a food processing company which has established its general capability against each clause of BS 5750 Part 2 and wishes to progress from there. We advise that you prepare similarly searching checklists for process or service control for use in your own company, following the lines indicated in Appendix 4.

5 Agreeing the audit programme

This is a matter of deciding who will conduct the audits, whether amendments to the checklists are for consideration, and discussing with the auditee the timing and the general nature of the forthcoming audit.

The audit is now ready to take place and should follow the system provided in Section 6.3 or one equivalent to it. Audit details are entered to the audit form provided in the Internal Quality Auditing Procedure. Corrective actions necessitated by observed nonconformances and agreed as reasonable by the auditee are listed in the audit nonconformance form and should be scheduled for completion within a reasonable time scale. The time scale should be acceptable to the auditee by providing sufficient time to order materials and services to carry out the work.

6.2   Training for quality auditing – the practical way

Trained internal quality auditors are essential for implementation of a quality system conforming to BS 5750. Auditing in the BS 5750 mode is quite specialised and failure to audit and record in the correct manner could cost you dearly on being assessed to BS 5750 by a Third Party Assessor.

Several consultancies afford two day courses on Internal Quality Auditing to BS 5750 and many companies avail themselves of them as they have a high success rate and they provide certification of qualifying delegates. A typical programme for such a course is as follows.

Introduction to Quality Assurance
Quality auditing
Audit life cycle
Preparation and planning
Conducting an audit
Making a checklist
Analysis of results
Conducting an opening meeting
Conducting a closing meeting
Corrective actions

Extensive use is made of role playing and case studies on these courses as it is difficult to address individual delegates' quality systems given that a typical class size is sixteen and the delegates drawn from various industries.

Some companies prefer audit training to be based on practical in-house auditing of their own operations under control of their own managers. They may previously have had one or two of them trained off site on a course of the type described above and will then employ them to conduct all audit training for their own company from that point.

For small companies unable to afford such courses, we suggest that, after studying this chapter and the checklists of Appendices 3 and 4, you should be well placed to tackle internal quality auditing to BS 5750, as the contents of this chapter are similar in intent to those of the above course. In this way you should be able to put a conforming internal quality auditing procedure to BS 5750 into operation.

The question arises whether studying this book and putting its advice into practical operation of your audits would, in itself, constitute 'training' in the eyes of assessors. There could be difficulties here as you would not be in possession of a certificate of training in internal quality auditing. On the other hand, as there is no written requirement in BS 5750 for externally conferred certification of audit training, you could consider either of the two options set out below.

1 Self certification, quoting this and other relevant texts as your source material.
2 If pressed by an assessor for externally conferred certification, you could consider inviting a trainer to visit your factory to fine tune your auditing system, assess the auditing capability of the participants in your audit programme and then 'certificate' them as trained auditors.

Small firms are advised to have at least their Management

Representative for BS 5750 and one other person trained in internal quality auditing. Larger firms should spread the net more widely to create an audit pool of appropriately trained people.

6.3   A model Internal Quality Auditing Procedure to BS 5750

The auditing principles outlined in this chapter have been embodied in a model internal quality auditing procedure to BS 5750 given in the following pages. We have found this slim procedure suitable for use in all firms we have worked with. As it is a 'generic' procedure, applying to all companies in much the same way, it has needed little adaptation to individual circumstances and is therefore offered in this chapter virtually ready for use except for formatting to BS 5750 (for details of this see Chapter 4).

After listing its contents, the operation of the procedure (numbered 16.1 to trace to Clause 4.16 of BS 5750, Part 2) is described in a few sentences. Quality Record 16.1.1 is used to record the conducting of the audit. Quality Record 16.1.2 is used to record nonconformances and to indicate corrective actions. One form 16.1.2 is recommended for each corrective action.

Quality Record 16.1.3 provides an audit plan for the forthcoming twelve months and invites entry of data to signify that successive audits have been planned, conducted, acted upon and closed out. More elegant versions of this spreadsheet can be created using computer graphics if desired but even in the skeletal form shown in Quality Record 16.1.3, the requirements of the Standard are met.

In Section 6.4 of this chapter details are provided of a specimen internal quality audit carried out using this procedure in which a typical nonconformance is noted and followed up appropriately.

Outline Internal Quality Auditing Procedure

Contents
1 Internal quality audits: organisation, control, recording and review

Appendices:

Quality Record 16.1.1
Quality Record 16.1.2
Quality Record 16.1.3

Internal quality audits: organisation, control, recording and review

The auditors:	Trained auditors from the company's pool of auditors.
Aims of the audit:	To audit functions and areas of the company's operation on a programmed basis for compliance with BS 5750.
Credentials of the auditors:	At least one manager has been formally trained in auditing to BS 5750 and has trained colleague auditors.
Frequency of the audits:	Monthly.
Organiser of audits:	The Quality Manager or Management Representative for BS 5750.
Planning of audits:	A forward audit programme is pre-announced to all affected area managers. Audit checklists are used as part of the plan.
Reporting system:	Audits are recorded on Quality Record 16.1.1.
	Nonconformances found during audits and remedial actions are recorded on Quality Record 16.1.2.
Review system:	Audits and follow up actions are reviewed, as a minimum, at the following Management Review Panel.

Specimen internal quality audit record:

Quality Record No. **16.1.1**   Retention period: **Two years**

TITLE: **INTERNAL QUALITY AUDIT REPORT**

Originator: _____

Date of issue: **1.1.93**   Issue number: **First**

If a reissue, reason for reissue: **N/A** _____

Authority for issue/reissue: _____

Audit report no: Date: Area/Function
                                                audited:

Auditors: Auditee(s):

Type of audit:

Relevant BS 5750 clause(s):

Observations:

Signed, auditors _____

Actions agreed: To be completed by:

Signed, auditee _____

Recommendations for follow up:

Signed, Audit Manager _____

Date:

Distribution: (list of people to receive this report)

Specimen internal quality audit corrective action report:

Quality Record No. **16.1.2**   Retention period: **two years**

Title: **INTERNAL QUALITY AUDIT NONCOMPLIANCE REPORT
WITH CONSEQUENTIAL ACTION**

Originator: _____

Date of issue: **1.1.93**   Issue number: **First** _____

If a reissue, reason for reissue: **N/A** _____

Authority for issue/reissue: _____

Audit reference number _____(For full details see relevant form 16.1.1.)

Noncompliance(s)

Signed, auditors _____

Signed, auditee _____

Recommended remedial action

Target completion date _____

Signed, auditors _____

Signed, auditee _____

Remedial action completion report:

Signed, auditors. _____

Approved (signed) by auditor_____ Date _____

Further comment (if any) by auditor:

Specimen internal quality audit plan:

Quality Record No. **16.1.3**   Retention period: **two years**

Title: **INTERNAL QUALITY AUDIT PLANNER**

Originator:

Date of issue: **1.1.93**   Issue number: **First**

If a reissue, reason for reissue: **N/A**

Authority for issue/reissue:

Annual schedule of BS 5750 compliance audits

Company: Year:

KEY: 1 = Audit planned   4 = Noncompliances corrected
  2 = Audit carried out and reported   5 = Audit closed out
  3 = Noncompliances agreed

Area/Function
audited   Months of the year

	Jan	Feb	Mar	Apr	May	Jun	Jul	Aug	Sep	Oct	Nov	Dec
Sales	1											
	2											
	3											
	4											
	5											
Purchasing		1										
		2										
		3										
		4										
		5										
Store			1									
			2									
			3									
Calibration				1								
Process 1					1							

(etc.)

6.4   Specimen internal quality audit to BS5750 Part 2 using the model procedure

The purpose of this section is to bring alive the internal auditing procedure of Section 6.3 by providing a worked example of an internal quality audit based on it. The example is a plant cleaning efficiency audit in a food processing factory although it could have been from any industry and it need not have been a process-related audit. The principles of conducting an audit should be clearly apparent from the example and it should be simple to carry them over into other situations.

The use of a specific checklist will be noted and the audit is based entirely upon it. A typical nonconformance has been invented, noted and followed up appropriately.

Note that no fault was found with the existing quality system in that the written procedures were clear and appropriate. The night cleaning shift were evidently carrying out their duties effectively as evidenced by favourable responses to items 12, 13 and 14 of the checklist. The single breakdown in the cleaning system was traced to a valve failure.

Effective short-term action has been taken and recorded on Quality Record 16.1.2/N22/1 and the plant engineer has been asked to keep the action of the valve under review following increased greasing frequency.

Specimen internal quality audit. Stage 1: recording the audit:

Quality Record No. **16.1.1**   Retention period: **two years**

Title: **INTERNAL QUALITY AUDIT REPORT**

Audit Report **No. 22**   Date: **10.10.93**

Area/Function audited: Efficiency of night shift plant cleaning and sanitisation

Auditors: Quality Manager; Microbiologist

Auditee(s): Prod Mgr; Deputy Prod Mgr; Night Shift Cleaning Supervisor

Type of Audit: A detailed site audit against the attached checklist PC1 (next page)

Relevant BS 5750 Clause(s): 4.9 (BS 5750 Part 2)

Observations: (Against the numbered items of the attached checklist PC1)

1 Yes; 2 Yes; 3 Yes; 4 Yes; 5 Yes; 6 Yes; 7 Yes; 8 Yes; 9 N/A; 10 N/A; 11 Yes; 12 No: there was evidence of cooked food residues inside the pipe connecting vessels A and B. 13 Yes: the two processes observed were being carried out to specification but item 12 indicates that a corner may have been cut in another part of the cleaning process; 14 Yes.

Signed, Auditors _____

Actions Agreed: The reason for the cooked food residues inside pipe A to B to be investigated and the problem solved.

To be completed by: Auditees in conjunction with plant engineer

Signed, Auditors _____

Recommendations for follow up:

As detailed on annexed corrective action report

Signed, Audit Manager _____ Date: **11.10.93**

Distribution:

Managing Director
Above Auditors
Above Auditees
Plant Engineer

Specimen internal quality audit. Checklist used for Audit No. 22

Internal quality audit programme: checklist No. PC 1
Plant cleaning and sanitisation

1 Is there a written procedure defining cleaning and sanitisation? Does it distinguish between cleaning and sanitisation?
3 Does it call for adequate post sanitisation rinsing?
4 Does it classify the company's methods of cleaning/sanitisation adequately?
5 Does it stipulate monitoring of plant hygiene, for example, by 'swabbing/culturing' or equivalent methods?
6 Does it list approved cleaning equipment?
7 Does it list approved cleaning and sanitisation chemicals?
8 Does it completely define the cleaning/sanitisation operations of the company?
9 If not, have further point of use Job Instructions been provided?
10 Are they available to all concerned?
11 Do they specify concentrations, times and temperatures as appropriate?
12 Does a tour of the factory indicate a well cleaned/sanitised plant?
13 Are cleaning/sanitisation schedules carried out as per Job Instructions? Check two processes while being cleaned.
14 Is there recorded evidence of good plant hygiene from lab records e.g. 'swab test' results? Check the records.

Specimen internal quality audit. Stage 2: acting on the nonconformance:

Quality Record No. **16.1.2**   Retention period: **two years**

Title: **INTERNAL QUALITY AUDIT NONCOMPLIANCE REPORT
         WITH CONSEQUENTIAL ACTION**

Originator: _____

Date of issue: **1.1.93**   Issue number: **first**

If a reissue, reason for reissue: **N/A**

Authority for issue/reissue: _____

Audit Reference No: 22 (For full details see relevant form 16.1.1)

Noncompliance: N22/1

An audit of the night shift plant cleaning/sanitisation efficiency on 10.10.93
revealed the presence of cooked food residues on the inside of the stainless
steel pipe connecting vessels A and B, indicating a breakdown of the system.

Signed, auditors _____

Signed, auditee _____

Recommended remedial action.

1 Investigate the cause of the system breakdown.
2 Consider whether there are wider implications for plant hygiene.
3 Rewrite the relevant part of the cleaning procedure if necessary.
4 Take other remedial action as may be necessary.

Target completion date 10.11.93

Signed, auditors _____

Signed, auditee _____

Remedial action completion report.

1 The plant is automatically 'cleaned in place' by pumping of detergent and
sanitiser solutions around it in a computer controlled sequence. Investigation
revealed a 'lazy' valve which failed to direct sufficient detergent to the pipe
connecting vessels A and B.
2 Judging by the success of the rest of the audit this is an isolated
incident with no wider implications.
3 No rewrite of the cleaning procedure is judged necessary but see para 4.
4 The 'lazy' valve incident is the first of its kind. Position discussed with manufacturer who recommends greasing moving parts once a week instead of
once a month. Recommendation adopted.

Signed, auditee _____

Approved (signed) by auditor _____ Date _____

Further comment (if any) by Auditor:

Appropriate remedial action taken. Plant Engineer please keep under review.

6.5   Management Reviews

Clause 4.1.3 of BS 5750 requires that a management review be carried out at intervals to check the effectiveness of the company's quality system to BS 5750. Records of these reviews must be kept. Management reviews are a good opportunity to review at senior level important quality matters such as:
– assessment of results of internal quality audits
– customer complaints
– nonconformances not involving customers
– corrective actions.

Ideally these reviews are chaired by the chief executive and are attended by managers or supervisors with direct quality responsibilities. The frequency of reviews is not stipulated by the Standard. Once per quarter or oftener may be appropriate when the BS 5750 system is running in. When the system is established and operating efficiently a lower frequency may then be suitable.

The basis of a slim but effective procedure for conducting and recording management reviews is given on the following two pages. The first describes the procedure. The second is an appendix which serves as a record of the meeting.

To convert these two pages to a conforming procedure you should adapt it to your requirements and provide it with a title page and amendment record and appropriate page headers as in Chapter 4.

Outline management review procedure

Objective and scope
To review the quality assurance system regularly to examine its continuing effectiveness in light of changing circumstances. This procedure specifies the procedures to be followed in conducting the review, agreeing any necessary changes and modifying the system.

Responsibilities
The Chairman is responsible for scheduling and chairing the review.
The Quality Controller is responsible for convening the meeting, circulating the agenda, providing information and recording the proceedings.
Staff, as defined in the Agenda for the Management Quality System Review, are required to attend.

Documentation for review
Management Quality Review agenda and minutes

Internal Quality Audit Reports
External Quality Audit Reports
Corrective Action Reports (including customer complaints)
Supplier Grading Records

Procedure
– The Chairman or delegate shall nominate the participants in the Management Review and decide on the frequency of meetings.
– The Quality Controller shall agree a generally convenient date with the designated participants and issue an agenda giving notice of the meeting.
– The Management Review shall embrace as a minimum:
review of actions arising from previous Management Reviews
Internal Quality Audit reports
External Quality Audit reports
Corrective Action reports
supplier/subcontractor performance
customer comments and surveys.
– The Chairman or immediate delegate shall chair the review and the Quality Controller shall record the proceedings and actions (with time scales for completion of actions). These shall be issued within five days of the meeting.
– Those actioned to implement changes shall do their best to complete them within stated time scales.
– The Quality Controller shall audit the changes as appropriate and report back on their effectiveness.
– Records of Management reviews shall be held for five years minimum.

Specimen management review record:

Quality Record No. **1.1**   Retention Period: **Five years**

Title: **MANAGEMENT REVIEW RECORD**

Originator: _____ Date of issue: _____ Issue number: _____

If a reissue, reason for reissue: _____

Authority for issue/reissue: _____

Date of meeting _____

Chaired by _____

In attendance _____

1   Review of minutes of previous meeting:

2   Current business:

(Enter all findings below. Use extension sheet if necessary and
annexe copies of relevant review data)

BS 5750 requirement	Current status of company against it	Action (if necessary) to come in line with requirement

3   Date of next management quality review:

4   Signed: _____ Chairman

Chapter 7

Corrective action

Contents of chapter:

7.1   Corrective action and related procedures

The undernoted clauses of BS 5750, Part 1 are interrelated and it is convenient to treat them as a group in this chapter. We suggest that corrective action (4.13) cannot be taken until we know the non-conformance (4.12). Identification and isolation of affected product cannot be effective unless there is efficient product traceability (4.7) and, where relevant, effective status indication of product (4.11).

The undermentioned clauses are reviewed in Section 7.2 in the order given below and the chapter concludes with a model Corrective Action Procedure in Section 7.3.

4.8   Product identification and traceability
4.12 Inspection and test status
4.13 Control of nonconforming product
4.14 Corrective action

7.2   Related procedures: traceability; inspection and test status; control of nonconforming product

7.2.1:   Control of traceability and product recall

This aspect is addressed in Clauses 4.8 of BS 5750, Part 1 and 4.7 of BS 5750, Part 2 headed 'Product identification and traceability'. Its main requirement is for companies, where appropriate, to establish procedures to ensure that their product is identifiable at all stages of production, delivery and installation. Where traceability is specified, product should be identified by, for example, a batch number.

Commercially, the requirements for product traceability have become more demanding in recent years and we suggest that it is in most companies' interests to install traceability procedures if not already in place. In some branches of industry, for example, food processing, healthcare and pharmaceutics, traceability is legally enforceable and has to be supported by a product recall procedure. This enables potentially dangerous product to be traced to and recalled from all locations such as shops and warehouses if demanded by the severity of the situation. Recently, traceability has been much improved by the widespread adoption of computer based stock control and distribution systems and by installation of ink jet printers for marking traceability information such as batch codes to product containers on-line, immediately after closure.

There is general agreement that computer controlled container coding by ink jet and related techniques is more legible and controllable than coding by more traditional methods such as embossing. Other things being equal, ink jet or equally reliable coding methods should be given preference over alternative systems. In some sectors of industry, for example, whisky bottling, ink jet coders are sufficiently sophisticated to mark sequential code numbers to bottles, so that each bottle is uniquely traceable to the exact time of bottling. This degree of container traceability is unusual.

Generally, container marking which affords traceability to a batch of product, or in the case of continuous processes, to a suitable time interval, is sufficient to meet requirements whether legally imposed or otherwise. No time interval is legally defined and may be as much as a day for certain continuous processes such as milk processing, where tanker loads of milk are pumped continuously to tanks and thence to a continuous process, with consequential loss of tanker traceability.

The two outline procedures in this section for traceability and product recall are based on continuous milk processing. The first describes traceability; the second addresses the product recall system that would be implemented if a serious product fault were discovered after product had been released to the trade. Traceability and recall are generally simpler and more definitive for batched processes if only because it is easier to mark batched product to trace to a specific batch. Suitable amendment of the following two procedures should be made to convert them from continuous to batch mode of production as necessary.

In branches of industry of relatively minor market sensitivity, traceability and recall procedures might not need to be in place or, if they are, might not be as rigorous as those employed by manufacturers of sensitive products. However they should be considered on their merits for each situation and instituted as necessary.

Outline traceability procedure for a typically large dairy operating continuous processing

Note that by the continuous mode of production, traceability to each day of production is the relatively modest aim of this procedure. Companies employing batch manufacture could mark and trace to each batch which might be much less than a day's production, depending on circumstances. Also note that because production is continuous the company cannot afford full traceability of their products to the ingredients used in their manufacture.

Marking and traceability of the company's manufactured products
Traceability to date of production is afforded for all of our cartoned products by means of a stamped or embossed date code or 'best before' date on each product container.

All bottled semi-skimmed milk is date coded on the cap and is traceable to date of manufacture.

Bottled full cream milk is not date coded, as there is no such legal requirement at present.

Pallet loads of the above are serially numbered, enhancing traceability so long as the goods are palletised.

Records of all vehicle loads and destinations are maintained as a further aid to traceability to source.

The following records are retained beyond the shelf life of all products and afford further traceability:
– daily production and quality records
– records showing materials in use each day
– pasteuriser time-temperature heat processing records.

Outline product recall procedure for the large dairy under discussion

Product recall
Product recall is facilitated by company procedures which define the marking and traceability of our products.

Factors suggestive of a need to recall product from the trade are immediately investigated at Board level with the support of the Quality Manager.

If recall is necessary the following plan is put into effect.

All customers supplied with the affected product are traced through records and immediately contacted by telephone or fax .

They are given full details of the product, the quantity supplied to them and the date code on the packages and asked to 'freeze' all affected product immediately.

Customers who further distribute our product to other sales outlets are also asked to trace the affected product to all destinations immediately and to 'freeze it'.

Our transport management, in close co-operation with our recall investigation team make immediate arrangements to call in affected product if necessitated by the severity of the incident.

If the company's investigation team judge that there may be a potential public health risk, appropriate authorities are urgently contacted by telephone or fax with full details of the incident.

The possible need to highlight the incident through the media is given full consideration and action taken as necessary.

The Quality Manager investigates all possible causative factors and, through the Product Identification and Traceability Procedure and other procedures and documents, takes all possible steps to define:
– the exact production period affected
– action required on raw materials and processes suspected of having caused the incident.

All affected product is returned as soon as possible to the factory. A full count of affected product is carried out and recorded.

7.2.2   Inspection and test status

This aspect is addressed by Clauses 4.12 of BS 5750, Part 1 and 4.11 of BS 5750, Part 2. The requirement is for material and product to be suitably identified at all stages to make it clear whether it has passed relevant tests and inspections. This can be met in various ways depending on the nature of a company's business. Three examples are considered below.

1 Route cards can be effective status indicators where work progresses through a series of operations to a finished product. The card should provide space for endorsement of the quality of work at each stage as it progresses and if possible should be secured to the work to identify it.

2 Mass production such as food canning cannot always be 'status marked' effectively. Pallets of processable materials and finished product present no identification problem. Neither do certain batch operations, for example, if canned foods are batch sterilised, steriliser crate loads can be tagged with heat sensitive cards which change colour on sterilisation thereby confirming sterilised status. With continuous sterilisation this would be impossible. In continuous processing it is frequently useful to address the requirement of this clause on the following lines.
   – All conforming process materials and product carry either

identification marks or labels showing their status or are identifiable by their in-plant situation in semi-continuous production within enclosed plant. Non-conforming product is segregated and marked 'quarantined'.
– Some industries, for example, pharmaceutics and healthcare have particularly demanding requirements for identification and status indication. All incoming materials are quarantined and labelled distinctively, for example, in red, to denote 'awaiting test and clearance'. When cleared, the red labels are partially over-labelled with white ones giving relevant clearance details.

Companies should be able to address their own particular needs on the above or similar lines according to the degree of status indication they need and the practicality of providing it in their operation.

7.2.3   Control of nonconforming product

The main requirements of the Standard for control of non-conforming product (Clause 4.13 of BS 5750, Part 1) are:
– procedures to isolate and effectively deal with substandard product or service
– responsible review and 'disposition' of such product
– request of customer 'concession' for use or repair of substandard product where specified in contracts.

These requirements are illustrated by the following draft procedures covering all three aspects. We believe there to be a case for a concession procedure even if not specified in contracts as it is only good business manners to draw potential problems to a customer's attention and invite their opinion on the acceptability of affected product.

The following outline procedures provide the necessary operational details but are not fully formatted to BS 5750, Chapter 4 provides the necessary formatting details.

The procedures are so generic in application that they could probably be taken into most manufacturers' systems with little amendment.

Procedure: Control of nonconforming product

Contents
Definition of 'nonconformance'
Procedure for dealing with nonconformances
Responsibilities

Definition of nonconformance
Any situation arising where a raw material, process, finished product or service fails to conform to the company's specifications or equivalent controls.

Procedure for dealing with nonconformances
The situation is immediately brought to the attention of the relevant supervisor or manager by the person detecting a nonconformance.

The aid of the Quality Controller or delegate is also enlisted.

Affected raw material and product are segregated to a designated area and labelled QUARANTINED for examination.

Processes and services are urgently inspected and if necessary halted pending further investigation.

During process investigations, careful consideration is given to the previous duration of the nonconformity and product suspected of being affected is quarantined.

The two officers listed above formally report the incident through the Corrective Action Procedure and complete a Corrective Action Report.

Responsibilities
All nonconformances are actioned by the relevant departmental supervisor or manager with the Quality Controller or delegate.

The Quality Controller or delegate is responsible for marking and identifying quarantined nonconforming product and for ensuring that it is traceable to a specific Corrective Action Report.

Disposition of goods affected by the nonconformance is the responsibility of the Quality Controller or delegate.

The Quality Controller or delegate is responsible for initiating and recording any remedial action to processes or operating methods necessitated by the Corrective Action study.

Outline procedure: review and disposition of nonconforming product

Contents
Responsibility for disposition of nonconforming product
Disposition review and decision making
Recording of dispositions
Appendix:
Quality Record 12.2.1: Disposition record for nonconforming product

Responsibility for disposition of nonconforming product
The Quality Controller, or in his absence his delegate, is responsible for all decisions on disposition of nonconforming product.

Disposition review and decision making
Nonconforming product is reviewed as in the procedure 'Control of Nonconforming Product'. There are four possible outcomes of the review. The product may be:
– reworked to compliance with specified requirements
– accepted for release with or without concession. If by concession, this is negotiated as in the customer concession procedure
– re-graded to an alternative application or sales outlet
– rejected or scrapped.

Recording of dispositions
All dispositions are recorded by the Quality Controller or Delegate on Quality Record 12.2 (a shortened form of which is given on the next page).

Outline procedure: Customer concession

Contents:
Explanation of the concession procedure
Basis of procedure
Operation of procedure
Appendix:
Quality Record 12.3.1: Concession request and progress record

Explanation of the concession procedure

Situations conflicting with quality arise from time to time. Sometimes they are not immediately rectifiable. Whether or not production/servicing/delivery may proceed under such circumstances is defined by this customer concession procedure.

In this company, a concession is a telephoned, written (or faxed) request from us to a customer for authority to proceed, with due control, in such 'out of specification' situations.

Basis of procedure
All out of specification situations are investigated by QA as they arise.

Where possible, each case is resolved by adapting it to conformity with specification, for example, by providing additional or

Quality Record No. **12.2.1**   Retention period: **two years**

Title: **DISPOSITION RECORD FOR NONCONFORMING PRODUCT**

Date: Product: Quantity:

Details of nonconformance:

Reviewed by: _____

Outcome of review:

Quantity reworked to compliance:

Quantity referred for concession: (Give reference number of concession report)

Quantity re-graded for alternative applications: (Give details):

Quantity rejected or scrapped:

Re-inspection of reworked product: (Give details)

Date:_____ Signed: _____ (Quality Controller or delegate)

improved materials, plant or labour, or by reworking to compliance.

Where adaptation and rework are impossible and the non-conformance is major the product is downgraded or scrapped. If minor, a concession is asked of the customer to authorise us to supply under the conditions of the concession.

Operation of procedure

This follows the path outlined in Quality Record 12.3.1, as follows.

The originator of the concession request initiates Quality Record 12.3.1, paras 1 to 4.

He/she contacts a 'concession review' panel comprising the BS 5750 Management Representative and at least one other appropriate manager.

The request is reviewed by the panel.

Alternative measures to a concession request are investigated and if feasible, adopted to rectify the situation.

Depending on the outcome of this investigation, the concession request is upheld or refused by the panel.

If upheld, the remainder of the procedure is implemented by the requester by completing paras 6 to 12 of Quality Record 12.3.1.

The concession request is then made of the customer with due urgency and if granted, is implemented and documented as in Quality Record 12.3.1 (a shortened version of which is given on the next page).

Quality Record No. **12.3.1**   Retention period: **Two years**

Title: **CUSTOMER CONCESSION RECORD**

Requester of concession:

Summary of request:

This should justify the request, explaining why adaptation to conformity with specification is impossible with available resources (attach report if detailed).

Customer/authority to be contacted:

Request upheld by Concession Review Panel? Yes/No

Signed: _____

If Yes, enter time and date of concession request:

How made: (Attach copy if written or faxed. Give summary if telephoned.)

Concession granted/refused/modified by customer? (Tick as appropriate. If modified give details. Attach copy of concession.)

Duration of concession:

Time/date concession implemented: _____ Signed _____

Special controls (if any) during concession:

Date concession terminated: _____ Signed _____

Brief final summary:

7.3   A model Corrective Action Procedure

This addresses Clauses 4.14 of BS 5750, Part 1 and 4.13 of BS 5750, Part 2, the main requirements of which are:
– nonconformances to be carefully analysed and recorded. Corrective action taken
– all relevant aspects of the business analysed to detect and eliminate nonconformances
– preventive actions taken and controls applied
– procedures formally changed to implement the results of corrective actions.

Again it is instructive to illustrate the above by means of a model procedure. The following outline procedure gives essential details except for page formatting for which you are referred to Chapter 4. The corrective action report annexed to the one page procedure is intended to serve for customer complaints as well as nonconformances detected in the factory.

Outline procedure: Corrective Action

Contents
Corrective actions: responsibilities and operation
Appendix:
Quality Record 13.1.1: Corrective action report record

Corrective actions: responsibilities and operation
Corrective action arising from nonconformance can be raised by any member of staff. It may result from audits, from reviews or from direct observation.

Corrective action may also result from nonconformance drawn to the company's attention from outside the company, for example in the form of a customer complaint.

In either instance, all means at the disposal of management and staff are used to correct the situation.

Responsibility for corrective action is with the Quality Manager or delegate.

He will analyse each situation with the help of appropriate staff and managers.

Details of the nonconformance are entered to Quality Record 13.1.1 and all subsequent action is recorded therein. Continuation sheets are used if necessary to give all relevant information.

Once a nonconformance is rectified, the Quality System is reviewed to seek a way of reducing/eliminating the risk of its recurrence.

A shortened version of Quality Record 13.1.1 is given on the next page.

Quality Record No.**13.1.1**   Retention period: **Two years**

Title: **CORRECTIVE ACTION AND CUSTOMER COMPLAINT
       RECORD**

Aim: To enable management to investigate all product non-
                conformances, whether originating within or outside the
                company, and to take full corrective action.

Format: As below, with all essential details entered (if necessary
                on an extension sheet).

Nonconformity:

Originator: Give full address if from outside the company (for exam-
                ple, a customer complaint).

Date notified: _____ Notified to: _____

To be actioned by: _____

Summary of investigation:

Established or suspected cause of nonconformance:

An isolated or a recurrent fault?

Action taken Give full details. (In the case of external customer
                complaints, give details, with outcome, of follow up
                action to satisfy the customer.) In all cases outline any
                consequential action that may have been taken to
                strengthen the quality system, including
                amendment/reissue of documents.

Date: _____ Signed: _____

Position in company: _____

Chapter 8

Sales and purchases

Contents of chapter:

Having examined in Chapters 3 to 7 the main generic aspects of the Standard (those applying to all companies in more or less similar fashion) we now move to those clauses of BS 5750 where individual companies' activities need to be carefully addressed in procedures which not only reflect their practices accurately but also conform to the requirements of BS 5750.

8.1   Control of contracts

This is covered by Clause 4.3 of both BS 5750, Part 1 and BS 5750, Part 2 headed 'Contract Review'. It is important to understand that 'contract' in this context means any sale transacted between a supplier and a customer, whether a contract for sale of a single commodity, or a formal, signed and witnessed contract defining a range of services or products to be provided to specified and agreed conditions of sale.

The word 'review' in the title of this clause is not used in the sense of a periodic, general review of the contract review procedure for accuracy – it means that every contract has to be scanned to ensure that:
a) the requirements are adequately defined and documented
b) any requirements differing from those in the tender are resolved
c) the supplier has the capability to meet contractual requirements.

Records of contract reviews must be held.

Requirements a), b) and c) of this clause have been embodied in the following excerpt from a typical Contract Review Procedure operated by a small company. Once again, for guidance, we have asterisked those parts of the procedure which address each of these requirements and have marked them with the relevant prefix letter from the above list, that is * a); * b) and so on.

Again we stress that the asterisks and letters would not carry over into a 'live' procedure – they are there only for the purposes of the text to check that all relevant controls have been incorporated to the system.

The procedure is an adaptation of one developed for a bakery but it could be readily adapted to other supplier/customer relationships.

Outline contract review procedure for a bakery

Contract initiation and review
Each order received from a customer constitutes a contract.

All supply of production and servicing from us to customers is to specification (* a).

Orders may be initiated by our customers in writing (by fax or by letter) or orally (for example, by telephone).

When we receive orders they are processed according to their mode of initiation as under:

Written orders
Existing customers (* a, b and c)

Each contract is reviewed for accuracy by one of the sales office staff against the customer's previous requirements, and for our ability to fulfil it. The accuracy review is carried out by comparing the contract against a retained copy (paper or electronic) of a recent comparable order received from that company. Discrepancies are queried with the customer by telephone and the contract altered to the customer's amended requirement if necessary. Written confirmation from the customer is requested in such cases. Our ability to fulfil contracts is formally verified with Production by the sales assistant for all orders exceeding £100 in value. For orders below that figure, ability to fulfil contract may be assumed by the person taking the order unless pre-advised by company management of capacity or other constraints on production, servicing or delivery.

New customers (* a, b and c)

On receipt of a first contract, a customer file is opened and forms the basis of subsequent contract reviews. The contract will only be executed when we have confirmed our ability to meet all its requirements.

Oral orders
Existing customers (* a, b and c)
A written order is raised by us for each oral order and 'read back' to the customer for accuracy. If the customer sends a written confirmation, our version is compared with it for accuracy and any discrepancy clarified with the customer. The arrangements of paragraph e for verifying our capacity to fulfil the contract also apply.

New customers (* a, b and c)

Note is taken of new customers' telephoned orders then they are asked to confirm them in a written contract. Our ability to fulfil contract is verified as above.

Sales specifications

Our purchasing specifications for our 'Stockist' controlled products serve as sales specifications.

Our specifications for our manufactured products also serve as sales specifications except that additional customer requirements may be noted to them as necessary.

Note that some companies have contractual obligations which are much more complex than those addressed by the above outline procedure for a fairly straightforward situation. For example they may have to prepare comprehensive tenders which, if secured, will each generate a file to which all relevant details are added as the contract progresses. Amendments to the original contract might have to be negotiated with the customer under concession, as defined in Chapter 7, in light of events which might be beyond the control of the manufacturer such as discontinuity of supply of a specified component. These and any other variations would have to be addressed in their Contract Review procedure.

8.2   Control of purchasing

This company function is covered by Clauses 4.6 of BS 5750, Part 1 and 4.5 of BS 5750, Part 2. Requirements are laid down for:

a) purchase to specification and verification that product supplied is as specified

b) assessment of subcontractors such as suppliers of materials and services

c) listing of approved subcontractors

d) clear purchasing documents

e) provision to the customer, where specified in the contract, the right to verify at source or on receipt that purchased product conforms to specified requirements. This situation may not arise in every manufacturer's operation but there should be a statement in your procedure that this facility is on offer to customers.

A separate clause of the Standard, 4.7 of BS 5750, Part 1 and 4.6 of BS 5750, Part 2 addresses requirements for verification of 'purchaser supplied product', that is material supplied by a customer to a manufacturer on free issue for incorporation into the customer's product. Such supply does not arise in every company's business.

When it does so, it can often be addressed in a short definitive statement in the Master Quality Manual along the lines indicated in Appendix 1 without the need to write a detailed procedure. For convenience, a typical complying statement on control of purchaser supplied product is repeated here.

Purchaser supplied product

Certain customers supply materials for use in their products only, for example packaging materials marked with their own print.

Such materials are treated as if we had purchased them and are subject to the same checks on receipt, the same preservation in storage and the same tests of function.

At any stage where customers' material shows nonconformity it is quarantined and the situation reported immediately to the customer.

Purchaser supplied material is pulled into our system of stock control.

Purchaser supplied material is stored in a manner that enables it to be readily identified.

To return to purchaser by a manufacturer of his own materials and services, a comment on paragraphs a) to e) from the beginning of this section is appropriate before examining the outline of a typical purchasing procedure to BS 5750.

a) Specifications
Most manufacturers operate on the basis of specifications for control of at least the underlisted aspects of their operation:
– process raw materials
– processes
– finished products.

Whereas it is normally possible to write clear process and finished product specifications (because they are largely under the manufacturer's own control), we suggest that manufacturers consider leaving themselves a degree of flexibility with raw material specifications.

For example an importer of rice may draw up a specification defining source, variety, grade, and post-harvest treatments but find that circumstances oblige him to purchase on the spot market from time to time. Such variation from specification is by no means uncommon and is encountered in most branches of industry. Therefore cover yourself with a statement in your specification giving freedom to spot purchase material of equivalent nature and quality, or words to that effect, provided that such material is compatible with your process and finished product specifications.

Also, ensure that your finished product specifications are meaningful and in general use. If you are in general chemical supply for example, check whether you may have carried irrelevant data from a demanding BPC or equivalent specification into any of your own product specifications, for example, if it states in the small print of a chemical you supply that it contains less than 0.1 ppm of lead and arsenic, there is an onus on you to verify supply of product to that standard even if such a standard of purity is unattainable by you and unnecessary to the customer. Such anomalies can be resolved by consultation with the affected customer who should sanction their removal from specification if unnecessary to his requirement.

b) Assessment of subcontractors

We suggest formalising (but not over formalising) subcontractor assessment by means of a pointage grading system as indicated in the following draft purchasing procedure. Remember that subcontractors as used in this section of BS 5750 includes suppliers. To avoid overcomplication, it is suggested that you restrict your supplier assessment grading to suppliers of processable materials before considering whether you may need extend it to other materials such as major office supplies. For small to medium scale companies we recommend that they adopt rapid, subjective (but fair and realistic) pointage grading of subcontractors. Larger companies might wish to use more formal systems.

c) Listing of approved subcontractors

This is sometimes overlooked by companies preparing for BS 5750. It is provided for in the following procedure.

d) Clear purchasing documents

Purchase order forms should be designed to enable all the required information to define a purchased material to be clearly identified. This need not entail lengthy entry of details as a purchased item may be clearly identifiable against a specification number or equivalent marking. The addressee should be clearly identified and price, delivery and any other relevant details marked to the order form.

Your purchasing procedures should leave you the freedom to place urgent orders by telephone but you should confirm them by fax or other hard copy.

e) Affording the customer the right to verify product at source

We have found it prudent to quote Clause 4.6.4 of BS 5750, Part 1 verbatim in the Quality Manual even if the situation is unlikely to arise in a company. Absence of the statement may be deemed a nonconformance by an assessor.

The foregoing requirements have been embodied in the following outline draft purchasing procedure for a bulk cereal processor except for paragraph e) above which is addressed in the Quality Manual of Appendix 1. Immediately after the undernoted purchasing procedure for a cereal processor, the gist of the same company's procedure for assessment of subcontractors is provided.

Outline purchasing procedure for a cereal processor

Raising a purchase order

Format: A standard purchasing form is used for all process consumables.

Processing purchase orders

– Only the undernoted may raise a purchase order for consumable materials affecting product quality, for example, cereal treatment chemicals:

(List names)

– All essential information to specify the goods ordered must be entered as in the specimen order form.

– A copy of each order is retained as a record and as a means of checking the order when delivered.

– Telephoned orders are recorded in writing and follow the above system.

– Orders placed by fax, etc., follow the above system.

Confirmation/inspection of purchased process consumables

– On receipt by the company, all process consumables are checked against their advice notes and the retained copies of the purchase order.

– The goods are inspected for compliance with specified requirements.

– If fully conforming, they are assigned a raw material stock control number and accepted to store.

– If nonconforming, the goods are quarantined, the supplier contacted and the goods are disposed of as appropriate following analysis of the situation by the Quality Controller or delegate.

Approved suppliers and subcontractors

Our suppliers of process consumables and our subcontractors for growth and supply of cereals have been formally approved and are listed.

Outline supplier/subcontractor assessment procedure for a cereal processor

Definition

For this procedure 'supplier' means a supplier of process consumables other than cereals. 'Subcontractor' includes growers of cereals, calibration engineers and pest control companies. Subcontractors and suppliers taken on to the company's approved list are required to satisfy assessment criteria outlined in this procedure.

Supplier assessment

The minimum requirement for a supplier is satisfactory completion of a detailed quality questionnaire.

Further requirements, some of which by their nature may be deferred, are:
– evidence of satisfactory previous record of supply to the company
– willingness to develop their quality system to an appropriate externally validated standard
– conformity to appropriate standards if audited at their site by officers of this company.

Listed suppliers are subject to routine grading on a points system against five criteria: quality; price; delivery; overall reliability; validity of their quality system.

A maximum of twenty points is awardable against each criterion.

Suppliers are awarded a grade ranking according to their total score on the points system as under:
– Grade A: 85 to 100 points
– Grade B: 70 to 84 points
– Grade C: 55 to 69 points
– Grade D: below 55 points.

The significance of these gradings is:
– Grade A: Fully approved. Goods on minimum inspection level
– Grade B: Commercially acceptable and reliable; Goods on 'average' inspection level
– Grade C: Borderline. Must improve. Goods on tightened inspection
– Grade D: Rejected. De-listed till significantly improved.

Suppliers are informed of their current grading status on request and also when their status alters.

Records of suppliers' gradings are maintained.

Suppliers' gradings are reviewed under the Management Review.

Assessment of subcontractors

– Cereal growing subcontractors are under close surveillance by the company and are assessed on the degree of conformance of their cereal consignments to specified quality tests.

– Significant failure of consignments to conform, for reasons judged by us to be within the control of the subcontractor, constitute grounds for removal of a subcontractor from our approved list.

– A pointage assessment system of the type described for suppliers is not appropriate for cereal subcontractors. Consistent conformance to quality specification is the prime requirement.

– Subcontractors providing services such as pest control and instrument calibration to the company are subjectively assessed on the efficiency of their service.

– Our list of approved subcontractors is reviewed under the Management Review.

Chapter 9

Processing and related functions

Contents of chapter:

This chapter examines the controls companies are required to apply to their processes and related functions such as inspection and the calibration of instruments used to control processes.

9.1 Process control

This aspect is addressed in Clauses 4.9 of BS 5750, Part 1 and 4.8 of BS 5750, Part 2 headed Process Control.

The prime requirements are for the following.
a) Well documented work instructions for all operations where their absence could cause quality problems.
b) Suitable plant and working environment.
c) Compliance with defined reference standards and equivalent.
d) Adequate process monitoring.
e) Approval of processes and equipment.
f) Definition of standards of workmanship 'to the greatest practicable extent'.

There is also reference to a requirement for tightened monitoring and control arrangements for 'special processes' as defined in the Standard. As the definition of special processes in the Standard is open to individual interpretation, we have never found it helpful to try to categorise companies' processes into 'special' or otherwise. There are too many borderline cases. The important thing is to provide adequate controls for all processes according to their nature. For example, it is academic to debate whether continuous thermal sterilisation of liquid foods in specialised plant is or is not a 'special process' as meant or implied, by BS 5750. What is important is to provide:

– appropriate plant controls for the critical variables in the process such as temperature, pressure and product flow rate
– recorded monitoring of such variables
– recorded testing of the raw and finished product.

Companies' responses to paragraphs a) to f) above are influenced by individual circumstances. It is instructive to examine their impact on two contrasting companies – a large company manufacturing heat processed packaged foods and a small company making products requiring manual skills. The former would almost certainly have had a sophisticated documented quality assurance system in operation before embarking on BS 5750 whereas the latter would be unlikely to have had one. Therein lies the difference in our suggested approach to the two companies' process control provisions in the following notes.

These notes are intended to serve as the basis of a conforming process control system to BS 5750, Part 2 for each company. Companies not operating in either food or in products requiring manual skills should also find the notes useful as the principles carry over into most situations.

Process control to BS 5750 for a large food processor

Such a company could find it profitable to audit its pre-BS 5750 provision of process control documents and decide whether their adaptation to BS 5750 should be major, minor or even unnecessary. The process control checklist of Appendix 3 would make a good starting point and could be later supplemented with the more searching process control checklists of Appendix 4, modified as necessary to individual requirement.

We list below our typical provision of process control procedures for food processors, which address the Due Diligence and related food safety requirements of *The Food Safety Act* 1990 and also seek to comply with BS 5750. Brief explanatory comments are provided with each. As the company's processes are quite complex, and the food processing industry is controlled by a mass of legislation, process control for the food industry is often heavily documented. This contrasts with the ensuing example of a flooring company, whose processes are definable by only a few procedures.

As only the procedure titles and explanatory notes are given below, it is worth recalling that each procedure, as well as describing a company practice, either provides work instructions and quality records as appendices or otherwise identifies them, for example, by reference to them in the text.

This list of process control procedures is indicative only and can be altered to individual requirement. It should prove useful to food processing companies starting from scratch and to those planning a major re-write of their existing process control manual to align it more formally to BS 5750. To companies whose pre-BS 5750 process control manual already addresses the points covered by our outline procedures 8.1 to 8.18 we suggest that they leave them unaltered. If lucid, clearly identified, formally originated and conforming to the requirements of BS 5750 for process control, why change?

The list of procedures and notes should also be helpful to companies in both the manufacturing and service industries with process controls as rigorous as those of the food industry which demand compliance with regulations and codes of practice. Manufacturers of pharmaceutics, healthcare products and speciality chemicals and professional service providers such as hospitals and dentistry practices should find them useful.

Range of operating procedures and guidance notes defining a food manufacturer's process control

8.1 Title: Good Manufacturing Practice and Due Diligence Compliance Protocol. Suggestion: State exactly how you meet these obligations in a series of short paragraphs.

8.2 Title: New Product Development. Suggestion: Outline your stage by stage procedure from bench top to factory scale highlighting how legally enforceable requirements are met.

8.3 Title: Selection and Commissioning of New Equipment. Suggestion: List and justify the selection criteria you adopt and the commissioning procedure you put major new plant through.

8.4 Title: Plant Maintenance. Suggestion: Describe how maintenance is requested; operated; recorded. Use the accumulated maintenance request and action reports as a means of controlling quality costs.

8.5 Title: Plant Cleaning and Sanitisation. Suggestion: Give a summary of your company's scheme and back it up with individual cleaning instructions.

8.6 Title: Control of Personal Hygiene. Suggestion: Summarise your controls, particularly in light of the new training demands of *The Food Act* 1990.

8.7 Title: Product Protection. Suggestion: List the devices and techniques you use to prevent product contamination from the environment, including process machinery. Devices may include metal detectors, sieves, guards, magnets and so on.

8.8 Title: Good Housekeeping. Suggestion: Briefly describe how you operate housekeeping, such as clean as you go and mobile housekeeping patrols.

8.9 Title: Pest Control. Suggestion: List the arrangements that apply in your factory. List approved subcontractor(s).

8.10 Title: Bar Code Verification. Suggestion: Describe arrangements and responsibilities, for example, who is responsible for verifying accuracy – you or your packaging supplier?

8.11 Title: Product Shelf Life Evaluation. Suggestion: Describe your system for ongoing shelf life review of products.

8.12 Title: Control of Specifications. Suggestion: List all your process control specifications and ensure that they are available to all concerned at their place of work. They are definitive 'work instructions', subject to regular review.

8.13 Title: Control of Sterilisation Processes. Suggestion: Ensure that you have definitive work instructions, for example, retort operation, hydrostat operation and so on. Suppliers' manuals can form an important element of this process control procedure.

8.14 Title: Control of Low Temperature Storage. Suggestion: An overview of your procedures for controlling materials and products stored at chill room and cold store temperatures.

8.15 Title: Control of Product Filled Weights. Suggestion: Give a description of your system for sampling and verifying conformity of products with *The Weights and Measures Act.*

8.16 Title: Control of Package Integrity. Suggestion: Summarise arrangements for sampling and verifying container seal integrity and code legibility.

8.17 Title: Waste Control. Suggestion: Describe arrangements for removal of solid and liquid food wastes and other forms of waste such as packaging waste.

8.18 Title: HACCP. Suggestion: If you operate HACCP (Hazard Analysis of Critical Control Points) describe your system.

Process control to BS 5750 for a small company making products requiring manual dexterity

The companies we have in mind here are joiners, plumbers, manufacturers of orthopaedic appliances, dental technologists, shopfitters, small scale engineers and the like.

The requirements of these companies for documented process control procedures are usually much less than the requirements of the large food processor just reviewed. Their main need is for skills of hand, eye and mind allied to the commitment to carry out a job to a specified standard (which may be a sample to be matched and not a drawing or a specification). Typically, such skills are developed through apprenticeships and day release education and reinforced by practical on job training and work. The education is highly practical and designed to impart skills that develop a youngster stage by stage to full tradesman status.

Such companies do not turn to operating procedures to tell them how to cut a mortise and tenon joint; how to mould a denture to a patient's mouth cast; how to weld two pieces of metal together. They must nevertheless address the Process Control clause of BS 5750 appropriately. It is tempting to consider doing so by making a brief statement in the process control page of the Master Manual to the effect that 'all of our work is carried out by skilled tradesmen, assisted as necessary by semi-skilled operators and working to appropriate specifications, samples, models or drawings'.

True as this may well be, it is likely to fall short of BS 5750 assessor's expectations. We suggest that there are few operations that cannot be made clearer by writing a short range of simple procedures defining key operations in simple stage by stage terms. Reasons for doing so are:
– the more easily incoming assessors can grasp the principles of the operations they are about to assess, the better. Your operations may be self evident to you but to an outsider they may not be
– simple operating procedures defining your key processes can form an excellent training package
– the very act of writing your own simple procedures concentrates the mind and can open the way to constructive change.

Therefore we make no apologies for introducing a few simple procedures to small, manually oriented companies. The key words are few and simple. As in the previous example of a large food processor, we list the process control procedures we consider appropriate to define the company to BS 5750. The contents page of each is given to indicate the essentially practical aim of the company's process control procedures.

The example is a small carpet installation company where are only six procedures, in sharp contrast to the number suggested for the food processor. The first three address principles, toolkit maintenance and floor preparation in a page or two. The final three describe the controls exercised during installation of the three types of carpeting installed by the company.

List of process control procedures defining a flooring company

Procedure 8.1:   Principles of flooring installation
Contents
1 Pre-treatment and conditioning of materials
2 On-site verification of materials
3 Preparing the job on-site
4 Carrying out the job
5 Inspecting the finished job

Procedure 8.2:   Toolkit maintenance
Contents
1 List of essential tools for operatives
2 Responsibility for maintenance of tools

Procedure 8.3:   Floor preparation
Contents
1 Damp proofing
2 Preparing concrete subfloors
3 Preparing timber subfloors
4 Preparing terrazzo, marble and similar materials
5 Preparing asphalt subfloors

Procedure 8.4:   Installation of sheet and tile flooring
Contents
1 Damp proofing
2 Preparation of concrete bases and screeds
3 Selection and use of underlays
4 Selection and use of flooring materials
5 Selection and use of adhesives

Appendices:
1 List of approved underlays
2 List of approved flooring materials
3 List of approved adhesives

Procedure 8.5:   Installation of textile floor coverings
Contents
1 Preparation of base
2 Damp proofing
3 Preparation and use of underlays
4 Preparation and use of adhesives
5 Planning the layout
6 Installation

Procedure 8.6:   Installation of carpet tiles
Contents
1 General floor preparation
2 Tools required
3 Measurement
4 Tightness
5 Cutting
6 Alignment
7 Installation

9.2   Control of inspection and testing

This function is addressed by Clauses 4.10 of BS 5750, Part 1 and 4.9 of BS 5750, Part 2. The key requirements are listed below with explanatory comments.

a) Receiving inspection and testing

The basic requirement is for incoming processable material to be inspected or otherwise verified for conformity with specification before use. Ideally it should not be used until verified correct. It is instructive to consider how this applies to large and small companies.

Large companies
Formal inspection and testing are routine practices for large companies and their procedures may well have been in conformity with the Standard before development of their quality system to BS 5750. Some companies, by the nature of their business, may go beyond the basic requirements of BS 5750 by carrying out pre-delivery quality control tests on processable raw materials.

Many food processors appoint field officers to liaise with farmers and carry out ripeness tests on crops before delivery to the factory. The 'tenderometer' for example, a mechanical device for assessing the texture and ripeness of peas in the field, is in regular use for predicting their optimum harvesting time, which is often critical within hours. In this way the company verifies the quality of product *before* receipt.

Pre-delivery verification may also be available to manufacturers from certificates of conformity and certificates of analysis provided by their suppliers. Large companies generally supplement this information with further tests on materials before accepting them for use. Such additional verification is mandatory upon manufacturing chemists under *The Medicines Act*. Most food processors also carry out additional laboratory tests on receipt of chilled perishables such as tanker loads of fresh milk. Large companies in other industries may have similar arrangements for formally testing materials on receipt.

Small companies

Small companies do not normally have the resources or the need to carry out formal testing of supplied materials, particularly if they purchase a wide range of them. They may instead rely on suppliers' certificates of conformity for verification of their process raw materials, supplemented by visual examination for 'fitness for purpose' and verification of delivery notes on receipt of the goods. As it is not always practicable to secure certificates of conformity, it is worth noting that product identifiers such as labels on the product containers can serve the same purpose if they are clear and definitive.

Small firms purchasing a range of branded materials for use in their products might well rely on the undernoted as a simple receiving inspection routine. Provided it is clearly stated in the company's documented quality system as their inspection procedure and provided the system works well for them and gives them the necessary assurances, BS 5750 does not deny them this interpretation of verification.

Simple receiving inspection scheme for a small company with no externally imposed requirements for formal testing on receipt

1 Delivery visually inspected for overall integrity.
2 A number of samples visually examined for correctness of data on label and for suitability for purpose.
3 Accuracy of delivery note verified.
4 Goods accepted for use.
5 Identified by marking with a code number for isolation if found nonconforming in use.

Preferably there should be a dedicated area for quarantine of nonconforming incoming materials but practicalities of space often preclude this. In such instances, an area should be set aside for temporary storage of such material which should be clearly labelled as nonconforming and isolated from sound stock as long as it is under quarantine.

b) In process inspection and testing

Large companies

Large companies will generally have had formal process control in operation before adapting their system to BS 5750. To them we have nothing to add that they will not already know and have in place, beyond a possible need to ensure that their inspection documents are appropriately headed and paginated and are under demonstrable issue and control.

Small companies

We have encountered small companies who have had to sharpen their in-process inspection and testing to meet BS 5750. A common deficiency is failure to formalise matters. Operatives may well be inspecting their own work and satisfying themselves on its quality before passing it to the next stage but that is not necessarily sufficient to meet the demands of the Standard.

There should be formal verification of approval of subassemblies and work in progress even if it is only by means of a tick or initials on a checklist. Ideally such verification should be by an inspector not carrying out the work but in the smallest firms who cannot afford even one inspector, operatives can be trained to impose 'self verification'. Provided such schemes are well devised and able to demonstrate effective control of process quality, they should satisfy assessors to BS 5750.

'Route cards' are sometimes beneficial as process controls in small firms in which work progresses through a series of operations to a finished product. A well devised route card, with space for endorsement of the quality of each stage as it is satisfactorily completed, is worth considering in those situations.

c) Finished product inspection and testing

Large companies

Many large companies operate a system of 'positive release', thereby meeting the requirements of BS 5750 for finished product release. Positive release implies that product is held by the manufacturer or a subcontracted warehouse until all quality test data relating to it have been verified as complying with specification. In some branches of industry positive release is formalised into a 'signing off' procedure whereby a responsible person must scan all test data on product and process before releasing each batch or equivalent of product under signature.

Circumstances may force some companies to release product on available evidence when it is impracticable or impossible to operate full positive release. For example perishable biological products cannot always await the results of laboratory incubation tests and will be released from the factory (although not necessarily to a customer) on the strength of complying raw material and process records supported by such finished product data as may be available.

Previous finished product incubation records will also form part of their release procedure, as consistently clear historical records indicate a strong quality assurance tradition in a company. Effective product traceability and recall procedures (Chapter 7) would enable defective product to be 'frozen' should there be an unexpected problem on final incubation.

Small companies
We see no difference in principle between the obligations placed on small companies for final product clearance compared with those for large ones. All relevant data should be verified correct before releasing finished product in small manufacturing companies even if their quality assurance system may be less elaborate than that of a larger company.

Service companies sometimes have difficulty satisfying BS 5750 assessors with their final job clearance procedures as there may be difficulties not present in a manufacturer's operation. For example when completing an installation job it is not always commercially attractive for the supplier to invite the customer's clerk of works to carry out a detailed pre-acceptance inspection of it as it may well lead to expensive rework, not necessarily all of which is within contract.

Service companies do, however, meet the spirit of this clause if they institute their own final job clearance checking procedure, ensuring that it is both realistic and in regular operation.

Companies, especially small ones, are reminded that inspection and test records should be held, to give evidence that product has passed all relevant tests before release. Such records need not be voluminous and at simplest could be route cards or equivalent as discussed on page 106.

9.3   Calibration

Clauses 4.11 of BS 5750, Part 1 and 4.10 of BS 5750, Part 2 lay down in very specific terms, in a series of paragraphs labelled a) to j), requirements for control, calibration and maintenance of equipment used in inspection, measurement and testing of product and processes. This is a particularly searching and specialised clause of the Standard which is reviewed by means of drawing on our experience of instrument verification in several contrasting industries.

– Identify the processes and tests which need critical control.

– Establish and write down the degree of control needed for each. It might be to within plus or minus one degree Centigrade for a critical sterilisation process. In that case a thermometer controlling sterilisation would almost certainly have to be accurate to plus or minus one degree Centigrade and to be calibrated to 'nationally traceable' standards.

– Identify the processes and tests which do not need critical control.

– Establish and write down the degree of control needed for each.

It might be wider than you first considered. For example a vapour phase chemical reaction might be controllable within quite wide limits: plus or minus 20 degrees Centigrade. If so, a plant thermometer at that location might serve an indicating function only and be under less stringent monitoring than the one used for sterilisation, particularly if the quality of the reaction product were regularly verified conforming by laboratory analysis. Steam pressure gauges on lines between boilers and apparatus generally serve an indicating function and can be maintained under less stringent monitoring rather than formal calibration.

– Categorise all relevant equipment into 'critical' and 'indicating' or words to that effect and list them.

– Determine and define a suitable frequency of calibration and monitoring for each item.

– Institute formal calibration and monitoring, where necessary engaging specialist help.

– List any calibration subcontractor(s) appointed.

– Label or otherwise identify the calibration status of each item.

– Keep all records of calibration and monitoring for a suitable period.

– Enter all relevant facts to a calibration procedure made available to all appropriate people.

– Address in the procedure action to be taken if an item of equipment is found to out of calibration. There could be product quality implications.

– Ensure that test and measuring equipment is properly handled and stored.

– Ensure that unauthorised adjustment of such equipment cannot be made.

– Supplement your formal calibration system for in plant instruments with routine, recorded visual confirmation of their continuing fitness for purpose.
– Be as generous as practicable in your selection of simple laboratory apparatus such as glassware. 'Certificated' burettes and pipettes for example are not much dearer than standard issue and the laboratory is generally an important part of the calibration programme.
– Get formal verification of all calibrations carried out, including signed assurance that specified limits were attained.
– Appoint a suitable person to control and review calibration and give him/her appropriate support and training.
– Formally audit and review calibration at defined intervals.

Having outlined general principles we conclude by quoting an excerpt from a particularly simple calibration procedure provided to a carpet laying company. This example indicates that although this clause of the Standard is demanding it need not result in an overcomplicated calibration protocol. The company were satisfied with the procedure and they passed assessment.

Excerpt from simple calibration procedure

The following test and measuring equipment is used by the company's operatives during floor laying operations.

Steel measuring tapes
They are used to take room measurements, to check room measurements on arrival at a work site and to measure the length of flooring materials once rolled out on site. They have a dual scale, inches and centimetres, and the smallest scale interval is 0.1 cm. That degree of accuracy is not required in practice. Room measurements are to 1 cm and flooring materials are first cut some 5–6 cm over dimension and finally cut to floor/room conformity during laying with no further measurement.

Folding rulers
They are used for taking preliminary rough measurements to within 1 cm.

Pocket hygrometers
These are used, under defined conditions, to give a preliminary rough reading of the relative humidity immediately above concrete screeds. Their scale displays relative humidity over the range 40 to 100% RH. The smallest scale interval is 5% RH.

Protimeter moisture meter
This is used for determining the moisture content of concrete screeds. Two holes are drilled in the screed to which the instrument's electrodes are inserted to a predetermined depth to give a rapid estimate of the moisture content.

Calibration of the above instruments
Measuring tapes and folding rulers
An accurate steel ruler of approved issue and graduated in 0.1 cm intervals over its length is retained in the Boardroom as a primary reference.
All working measuring tapes and folding rulers are calibrated against it once per year.
Working tapes and rulers are accepted for use and stamped or marked accordingly if accurate to within 0.25 cm over a 1m length.

Pocket hygrometers
They are calibrated annually at their most important working value, 75% relative humidity (RH), by sealing each in turn above a dish of saturated sodium chloride solution at normal temperature for at least one hour. The atmosphere above the dish should equilibrate at 75% RH and pocket hygrometers are accepted if within 8% of 75% RH under test conditions.

Protimeter moisture meter
This is calibrated annually by the instrument calibration company listed in the appendix.

9.4   Handling, storage, packaging and delivery

This aspect is addressed by Clauses 4.15 of BS 5750, Part 1 and 4.14 of BS 5750, Part 2 in a series of short paragraphs which clearly set out the requirements, namely that there must be appropriate controls for handling, storage, packaging and delivery backed by documented procedures. Each subject of this clause is addressed in this section.

Handling

Handling methods should be such as to prevent damage or deterioration of material and product. The Standard does not stipulate methods of handling which may be manual or mechanised. As it is in companies' commercial interests to handle their product appropriately, this paragraph is normally easy to address in a simple procedure outlining their handling methods.

Reference should be made in the procedure to methods in use for minimising material damage during mechanical handling, such as:
– use of plastic lined conveyor belts and chutes
– avoidance of excessive speeds, gradients and direction changes when handling materials and containers along trackways
– use of appropriate pump glands and seals to prevent lubricant penetration to liquid product
– careful manual handling of delicate items along assembly processes, for example, by conveyal in a trolley or basket or along a slow conveyor.

Fork lift drivers should be trained and 'certificated' and committed to safe driving and quality conscious material handling.

Where in use, product palletisation should be carefully controlled by training procedures, in writing as necessary, with the aims of:
– ensuring that only standard, serviceable pallets are used for storage and transportation of the company's finished goods
– defining pallet build to give a stable load
– defining overwrapping of pallet loads for security and stability
– defining whether one or more pallet loads may rest on another in store or transit.

Storage

Store environmental conditions should be noted to procedures and rigorously enforced for sensitive products, especially those stored in modified atmosphere or sub-ambient temperature conditions.

Such stores should be equipped with externally readable temperature and, if relevant, atmosphere recorders.

The use of store racking is advisable where appropriate.

Good housekeeping and pest control should be in operation in relevant industries and there should be adequate space allocation.

A first in, first out (FIFO) system of stock rotation should be enforced as appropriate.

There should be provision for segregating and identifying material and product which is nonconforming or undergoing examination.

Packaging

Procedures should state arrangements for packaging product. Depending on the industry and product this may need definition on three levels: for primary, secondary and tertiary packaging. These terms are illustrated with reference to food canning, for adaptation to other situations as required.

Primary packaging

This is the food container which is hermetically sealed to keep out air and bacteria after sterilisation and is subject to rigorous quality control for seal integrity. This must be carried out to a definite plan at a suitable frequency. Related data such as filled weights and container vacuum and 'headspace' follow a similar pattern of control because irregularities in them can impose strain on can seams and cause leakage and other problems.

Secondary packaging

This refers to collation of labelled cans to sales outers such as cartons or shrink wrap blocks. In high-speed, automated factories alignment of the cans with the wrapping or cartoning machinery is critical to prevent damage and line jams and should be subject to close control and maintenance.

Tertiary packaging

This is preparation of palletised or alternative bulk loads of secondary units and should again be carefully defined along the lines proposed for handling.

Companies with alternative packaging systems to the above should define them, however simple they may be, in a short procedure or statement. For example dental technicians who despatch their product by post to dentists should describe the packaging which affords protection in transit. Manufacturers of electronic equipment should state their procedure for final product protective packaging, annexing relevant protective and packaging material specifications to the procedure.

Delivery

Depending on contract, manufacturers may deliver product to customers in various ways such as:
– using their own vehicles
– using the vehicles of subcontract hauliers
– having it picked up from their premises by the customer.

In the last situation, responsibility for conservation of product quality in transit normally passes to the customer at the factory gate who must therefore ensure that the product is correctly packaged and in visually acceptable form before loading it to his vehicle.

In the first two cases, the manufacturer either has total responsibility for quality in transit (the first case) or he may have a shared responsibility for it with the haulier (the second case).

Written procedures should define the manufacturer's arrangements for delivery which can sometimes be complex by involving all three. There may be other special requirements such as air freight and shipping, both forms of subcontract haulage with special requirements.

Irrespective of method of transport, the manufacturer should ensure that all parcels conveyed in composite loads are clearly identifiable by labels showing the addressee and effectively segregated from each other, for example, by spin or shrink wrapping of each destinee's parcel as a separate unit.

Where special safety requirements have to be fulfilled, as in conveyal of bulk chemicals, appropriate training and instructions must be provided to drivers and goods and vehicles must bear appropriate 'Hazchem' and other markings.

Where subcontract haulage is used for foods and other sensitive products contracts with hauliers should contain appropriate clauses such as the following.

Vehicles and goods containers shall be clean, internally dry, of sound construction and in good repair.

Exhaust fumes shall not penetrate to the goods container whether the vehicle is moving or stationary.

Goods containers must be free of odours, taints and foreign material and contamination such as oil spillage.

Chilled goods containers shall be thermostatically controlled between zero and seven degrees Centigrade and equipped with a time/temperature recorder.

Goods containers should be dedicated to the product style defined in the contract.

Chapter 10

Quality records and statistics

Contents of chapter:

10.1   Quality records
10.2   Statistical control

By addressing the above aspects of BS 5750 this short chapter completes the analysis of all eighteen clauses of BS 5750, Part 2, each of which also applies to BS 5750, Part 1. A further two clauses, covering design and servicing and applying to BS 5750, Part 1 only, are addressed in Chapter 11 to complete the review of all clauses of the two parts of BS 5750 applying to manufacturers and service companies who do not specialise in inspection as addressed by ISO 9003.

10.1   Quality records

Essentially, Clauses 4.16 of BS 5750, Part 1 and 4.15 of BS 5750, Part 2 set out requirements for identification, storage and maintenance of quality records. The 1987 version of BS 5750 is non-committal on whether the records may be electronic or whether only hard copy is acceptable. We have so far encountered little evidence in small to medium companies of exclusively electronic capture and storage of active quality records generic to the BS 5750 quality system, for example, quality audits reports, training records, disposition records for nonconforming product and the like.

As there is no stated objection to electronic records in the Standard it may be assumed that in principle, companies could begin to save time and paper by storing at least some of their quality records on disk provided due attention is given to:
– appropriate training of people entitled to use the electronic system
– restricted access to sensitive disks by designated people, under control of keys, pass cards or personal codes
– unique identification of key people responsible for 'signing off' important quality actions such as product release
– the facility to print copies of electronically stored data as necessary

– adequate back-up facilities
– foolproof storage and protection of the system against damage
– operation of a hard copy system along with any intended electronic system for a trial period till full reliability of the latter is demonstrated.

In light of the previous paragraph, it would therefore appear to be in most companies' interest to start operating their quality records on the basis of hard copy even if they intended to convert to electronic storage later.

An outline procedure is given below to illustrate how control of quality records can operate in a representative company. The distinction drawn between the Group A and Group B records may not be meaningful in all operations. It is offered for possible adoption by companies, some of whose activities were controlled by detailed quality records (maybe externally imposed on them by regulatory bodies) before the company converted to BS 5750.

Outline quality record control procedure

Contents
Objectives and scope
Responsibilities
The company's quality records
Control procedure

Appendix:
Quality Record 15.1.1: List of quality records used by the company

Objectives and scope
Our quality records demonstrate effective operation of defined practices and ensure that the specified quality standards have been attained. The records are held for reference by staff, by customers and by independent assessors. All are retained for a specified duration (see Quality Record 15.1.1) in an orderly manner in a suitable storage environment.

Responsibilities
It is the responsibility of staff listed within operational procedures to ensure that appropriate quality records are originated and maintained. Amendments are through the Document Controller under SOP 4.1.

It is the responsibility of the Document Controller to compile Quality Record 15.1.1 and to keep it up to date.

Our quality records are listed in QR 15.1.1.

Procedure

Our quality records are identifiable to the service concerned, legible and able to demonstrate achievement of the required quality.

Our quality records are properly indexed, filed and maintained.

The retention period for quality records is listed in individual procedures or stated in QR 15.1.1. Our Quality Records divide into two groups.

– Group A: Quality Records recently issued and directly controlling key aspects of the BS 5750 quality system. These are formally headed and numbered to BS 5750.

– Group B: Quality Records which have been in use in the company for some years to control the company's processes. These are clearly marked as to purpose and will be considered for re-formatting as those of paragraph A as they come up for amendment and reissue.

Our quality records are available, on request, to customers and third party assessors.

When the stated storage period for quality records has expired and there are no further reasons for retaining them, they are destroyed by the Document Controller under control of QA.

Quality records are available through their retention period for problem analysis as may be required. This may lead to corrective actions under SOP 13.1, Corrective Action.

10.2   Statistical control

The relevant clause of the Standard, 20 for BS 5750, Part 1 and 18 for BS 5750, Part 2, states that 'where appropriate, the supplier shall establish procedures for identifying adequate statistical techniques for verifying the acceptability of process capability and product characteristics'.

In our view, by the wording of this clause, 'statistical' is intended to imply mathematically based statistical sampling and control systems of the kind used in statistical process control (SPC) and related schemes.

This is apparently a fairly widely held view as we see company quality manuals which address this aspect on the lines 'we do not apply mathematically based statistical control procedures but should the position change we will install appropriate systems'. Having addressed the requirement in the Master Quality Manual with this statement they then make no further reference to it in their documented quality system.

We have no problem with that approach to this clause and have made similar statements on behalf of clients in their Quality Manual with no adverse reaction from assessors.

However a word of caution is appropriate. Most mass production is controlled by sampling and analysis of process and inspection data. In fast moving processes generating hundreds of small items a minute, formal statistical schemes are likely to be in use. In such situations the statement in the manual would say so and there would be a case for a procedure or two to define the systems in operation.

The systems would probably be at least moderately complex, calling for measurement of critical variables at regular short intervals followed by calculation of trend indicators such as average, range, standard deviation and perhaps 'tolerable negative error', a term significant in Weights and Measures control to the 'averages' system. The data might be displayed on a control chart situated by the process for ready reference by process workers and inspectors. Alternatively an electronic control system might be in operation with all calculations performed on input of the data, with a print-out issued on pressing a button. In either instance the method should be described in an operating procedure.

A slight difficulty arises with slow moving processes sampled fairly infrequently and controlled very basically, for example, by measuring a key variable such as the length or weight of a single unit at intervals and recording each single observation on a simple chart with no further elaboration apart from indication of control limits within which conforming readings must fall. Is this a 'statistical technique'? Probably not by normal definition but it does no harm to mention it in the Quality Manual along the undernoted lines. We suggest that even so simple a process would merit a simple operating procedure or work instruction to define it.

Suggested wording in the Quality Manual to meet such as situation is: 'We employ only the most basic systems of recorded process control. They are suitable for our present needs but should circumstances alter we will install appropriate statistically based control systems. The present system is fully described in a work instruction'.

The work instruction or operating procedure could be a single page, appropriately originated and headed, stating exactly what happens on the following lines:
– a stamping is removed from the line every fifteen minutes
– its length and width are measured by Vernier micrometer to within plus or minus 2 mm
– the results are entered to a simple control chart (specimen

attached)
– the sample is accepted and the process allowed to continue if both readings are within the control lines.
– if one or both of the readings are on or outside the control lines the operator (or supervisor) is immediately informed and corrective action taken.

The position with subcontracted statistical services should not be overlooked, particularly by service companies engaging agencies to carry out market surveys and field research on their behalf. If such work is statistically based, for example, employing significance testing of responses from representative samples of the population, it should be explained in procedures.

Aspects of BS 5750, Part 1/ISO 9001: design and service issues

Contents of chapter:

11.1   BS 5750, Part 1 *v.* BS 5750, Part 2

Although both design and servicing are addressed by BS 5750, Part 1 (and not by BS 5750, Part 2) we suggest that it is in most companies' interests to examine how they stand on both issues and to make appropriate statements about them in their quality manual even if pursuing BS 5750, Part 2. There are few manufacturing and service companies without some degree of involvement in design and after sales servicing and the fact that they might have opted for registration to BS 5750, Part 2 instead of BS 5750, Part 1 may be a matter of preference rather than total absence of design and after sales servicing from their operations.

Some assessing bodies are quite directive about which version of BS 5750 companies should pursue and will press them to BS 5750, Part 1 if they perceive their design element as significant. Others are more relaxed about it and leave it to the client to opt for BS 5750, Part 1 or BS 5750, Part 2 as they wish. We prefer the latter approach for a number of reasons.
– The word 'design' is open to interpretation and different companies react to it in different ways. Some may in modesty view their design element as rather basic, not requiring great originality or innovative quality. Others may tend to overstate their design element somewhat, for example representing project control as design, because they may wish the prestige of registration to BS 5750, Part 1.
– Some companies may wish to leave design out of their registration and be perceived as primarily manufacturers or purveyors of a service.
– Some may wish to defer registration of the design function until they have gained registration to the rather less demanding BS 5750,

Part 2 for 'production and installation' only.
– Some may elect to address their design element under Clause 4.9, Process Control, of BS 5750, Part 2, if it is particularly product/process oriented and not unduly complex.
– Some may wish to cut assessment costs as it is cheaper to assess a company to BS 5750, Part 2 than BS 5750, Part 1. The 'design' interface between BS 5750, Part 1 and BS 5750, Part 2 is a grey area and should benefit from reappraisal under the planned review of BS 5750 leading to an intended reissue of the Standard around 1996.

Under the present definitions of BS 5750, Part 1 and BS 5750, Part 2, we recommend that companies with an appreciable design function should consider aiming for BS 5750, Part 1. We also suggest that those with a lesser design involvement and heading for BS 5750, Part 2 should not forget to address design somewhere in their quality system. Moreover, although not obliged by BS 5750, Part 2 to comment on their arrangements for after sales servicing we suggest that it may be in their interest to do so along lines indicated in Section 11.3.

The remainder of this section addresses design in terms of Clause 4.4, Design Control, of BS 5750, Part 1 and servicing in terms of its Clause 4.19.

11.2   Control of design

As stated, design requirements and perceptions of the word 'design' vary from company to company. So much so, it is difficult to illustrate the procedural requirements of BS 5750, Part 1 for design without basing it on a concrete example. We have chosen one from our own experience – delivery of consultancy assistance by our own small company to pharmaceutical companies for new product design to *Medicines Act* standards. The example has manufacturing and service elements because in the situation described we are in the role of service providers with the client as potential manufacturer. In the first instance we examine the manufacturer's design obligations under *The Medicines Act* and BS 5750, Part 1. That is the manufacturing element. We then provide the simplified version of a procedure we use to control the overall design of the consultancy input, including verification of product integrity and process capability to the manufacturer's requirements. That is the service element.

We trust that companies in other industrial and service sectors will find the guidelines illuminating and be able to convert them to their own situation.

11.2.1   Manufacturer's aspects of design control for a new drug

We have assumed the client company in the example to be planning manufacture of a simple drug, which although controlled by licence under the British *Medicines Act*, matches products already in the market and is not innovative pharmaceutically or medically. Innovative drug development is the preserve of multinational companies with all appropriate resources. Nevertheless even 'simple' medicinal products have to follow a rigorous design procedure.

The design obligations of the company are addressed against the numbered paragraphs and explanatory short texts of Clause 4.4, Design Control, of BS 5750, Part 1 as below. Statements in single quotation marks are from the Standard. Ensuing statements are our suggestions on how each requirement should be met in the situation under review.

General (4.4.1)
'The supplier shall establish and maintain procedures to control and verify the design of the product in order to ensure that the specified requirements are met.'

The 'supplier' means the manufacturer in this context. Quite apart from BS 5750, Part 1, a formal design protocol is demanded of drugs manufacturers by the British *Medicines Act* for their development, testing and licensing. In the UK this was defined until 1992 by a detailed procedure issued by the British Medicines Control Agency. From 1993 it was superseded by a document 'The rules governing medicinal products in the European Community, Volume II' which sets out a highly definitive product licensing procedure running to 174 pages which is mandatory upon the applicant and as such, fully suffices in our opinion as a design and development planning system meeting Clause 4.4.1 of BS 5750, Part 1.

The EC document demands that all licence applications be backed by detailed reports from pharmaceutical, pharmacokinetic and clinical experts and that full compositional, processing, packaging, storage and quality assurance details supplied must meet the requirements of the licensing authority.

Assuming this to be a pharmaceutical manufacturer's sole design involvement, the EC document would in our view undoubtedly meet the requirements of Clause 4.4.1 on their behalf apart from a possible need to write a short bridging procedure linking it to their company practice.

Major non-European countries are rigorously controlled by comparable procedures which in our view should also suffice as conforming design procedures to BS 5750, Part 1.

4.4.2   Design and development planning

'The supplier shall draw up plans that identify the responsibility for each design and development activity. The plans shall describe or reference these activities and shall be updated as the design evolves.'

This can be a simple procedure detailing who is responsible for each element of the above design and development system. In small companies it may all be handled by a single 'Qualified Person'. In larger companies there may be a number of quality assurance and regulatory affairs staff with a contribution to the system. In each case the responsibilities should be identified and updated as necessary. The system should also be updated as necessary.

4.4.2.1   Activity assignment

'The design and verification activities shall be planned and assigned to qualified personnel equipped with adequate resources.'

Few pharmaceutical companies should have difficulty with this clause unless underresourced, in which case they would have to re-examine whether key people were adequately qualified and resourced to undertake new product design and verification. BS 5750, Part 1 is quite searching in this area.

4.4.2.2   Organisational and technical interfaces

'Organisational and technical interfaces between different groups shall be identified and the necessary information documented, transmitted and regularly reviewed.'

Again, this is not normally a problem area in a well organised pharmaceutical company. However the effect of take-overs and closures in a recessionary period should not be overlooked and company organisation should be critically reappraised in such situations.

4.4.3   Design input

'Design input requirements relating to the product shall be identified, documented and their selection reviewed by the supplier for accuracy.

Incomplete, ambiguous or conflicting requirements shall be resolved with those responsible for drawing up these requirements.'

We suggest that the requirements of this and the remaining clauses of Clause 4.4 Design Control (Design Output and Design Verification) should be met by means of a procedure detailing checks and controls operating at all stages of the product design process from 'bench' to production and marketing.

As a guide we give below a deliberately simplified outline of a version we employ in a consultative capacity for product development work on behalf of small pharmaceutical companies. It would need considerable development for use in larger companies but may also provide the germ of an idea for them. Equally it could be of value to a consultancy or similar company providing a formally controlled design service to a client outwith the immediate circumstances described.

We stress that only the skeleton of the procedure is provided overleaf. A file is opened at the outset of each project. As the various stages of the outline procedure are completed, reports and summaries are entered to the file which eventually provides full product development traceability from inception to market.

11.2.2   Outline consultants' product design planner for manufacturer, from bench to market place

Careful examination and recording of each of the undernoted is required

1   New product proposal/Date/Proposer

2   Initial evaluation of proposal by consultancy
2.1 GMP aspects
2.2 Compositional aspects
2.3 Medicines Act aspects
2.4 Labelling requirements and design
2.5 Manufacture potential (for example, compatibility with existing plant)
2.6 Formulation guidelines
2.7 Packaging requirement
2.8 Initial action to be taken

3   Preparation/evaluation of samples of new product
3.1 Sample code: .... Date: .... Evaluation: for client
     For consultant:

3.2 What modifications are needed?
        For client:
        For consultant:

Note: Reissue this form for each successive new sample till finally approved then signify acceptance here

3.3. Sample approved for production trial:
                        Client: Consultant: Date:

4   Evaluation of production trial
4.1 Any snags/equipment deficiencies?
                        Client: Consultant: Date:
4.2 Any new plant required?
                        Client: Consultant: Date:
4.3 Product/process suitable for adoption by client?
                        Client: Consultant: Date:

5   Preparation of product/process specification
5.1 Specification fully definitive?
                        Client: Consultant: Date:
5.2 Client satisfied with product, process and specification?:

6   Further work (Medicines Act products only): Client please answer
6.1 Help needed by client with clinical trials or equivalent?
6.2 With product registration?

11.3   Control of servicing

As with Design Control, Servicing is featured in BS 5750, Part 1 (Clause 4.19) but not in BS 5750, Part 2. The servicing statement of Clause 4.19 briefly requires that where specified by contract, 'the supplier shall establish and maintain procedures for performing and verifying that servicing meets the specified requirements.'

Even without formal expression in a contract, most manufacturers and service companies with a sound customer relations policy will have afforded some measure of free after sales service to customers and clients as an expression of care and goodwill long before developing a quality system to BS 5750.

Even if developing a system to BS 5750, Part 2 (in which 'service' is not featured) they should consider describing these traditional goodwill arrangements in a brief policy statement in their Master Quality Manual to BS 5750, Part 2. They should then consider whether they have any contractually binding after sales servicing obligations and if relevant, comment accordingly in their Manual to BS 5750, Part 2.

In our view a suitable place to express these points in a Manual to BS 5750, Part 2 is as a tailpiece to Clause 4.9 Inspection and Testing, on the reasoning that after sales service can be viewed as a form of post release inspection/verification.

We recommend commenting in this fashion even if aiming for BS 5750, Part 2 as it is an important enhancer of customer relations by affording reassurance in principle that the responsibility does not end at the manufacturer's factory gate or immediately a service company has discharged its contract, albeit to BS 5750, Part 2.

If developing a system to BS 5750, Part 1 such requirements are mandatory under Clause 4.19 and should be addressed accordingly, although not necessarily any more rigorously than through the similar arrangements suggested by us for BS 5750, Part 2.

If contractually defined after sales servicing is complex and diverse (to meet the demands of a range of customers with different requirements), there would clearly be a need for a supportive servicing procedure or procedures. If such servicing is simple (or unnecessary as with the supply of many low price consumer goods to the mass market) a short statement in Clause 4.19 of the BS 5750, Part 1 Manual may suffice to meet the obligations of BS 5750, Part 1.

In some areas of the service sector, such as consultancy, there is a tradition of affording clients a measure of free service after official contract termination and the undernoted excerpt from a representative consultancy's Master Manual is probably fairly typical.

Excerpt from 'Service' clause of a typical consultancy Quality Manual

4.19   Servicing

4.19.1 Where servicing is specified in contracts between us and a client this shall be to plans and procedures devised by the consultancy and agreed with the client to ensure that servicing meets all specified requirements.

4.19.2 Where there is no such contractual requirement, the consultancy shall offer to monitor progress on installations or services provided to clients during at least one visit to the client after project termination. This shall be at no additional cost to the client except for recovery of basic expenses as may be requested, for example, for clients more than 100 miles from our office.'

One would not realistically expect to see paragraph 4.19.2 in the manual of a typical manufacturing company which would be more likely to be definable by paragraph 4.19.1 or a similar statement.

Equally, service companies affording a more tangible service than consultancies, such as car maintenance firms, dentists, surgeries and certain local authority servicing departments would, by the nature of their business, be much more likely to be definable in terms of para 4.19.1 than 4.19.2 which may be unrealistic in their situation.

BS 5750/ISO 9000 and the service industries: the key requirements

Contents of chapter:

12.1 Similarities between the manufacturing and service industries

At present BS 5750 does not distinguish between manufacturing and service companies. The undernoted document does however provide helpful guidelines to interpretation of the Standard by those in the service industries.

BS 5750: Part 8: 1981/ISO 9004–2: 1991

The 1987 version of BS 5750, current at the time of writing, is a direct evolution from the original 1979 version which was exclusively directed to the manufacturing industries. Even the 1987 version has a distinctly manufacturing tone. Around 1990, many companies in the service sector began to realise the benefits of an externally validated quality assurance system and recognised BS 5750 as a suitable vehicle for their aims.

Some found difficulty in adapting the 1987 version of BS 5750 to certain situations in the service sector. This was particularly the case with companies delivering service in a relatively abstract form, affording 'product' such as education, training, consultancy and legal services. Some found the product orientation of the Standard confusing and difficult to relate to their own activities. Doubts were even expressed in some quarters whether service could really be effectively addressed by a quality standard with such clear manufacturing origins.

Less difficulty was experienced by companies affording more tangible and measurable services such as car maintenance, transport, storage and street cleaning which were more directly comparable with manufacture by being product related and therefore easier to express in terms of BS 5750.

Many companies in the service sector found translation of BS 5750 to their own quality requirements achievable by regarding the 'manufacturing' tone of the current BS 5750 as a semantic problem to be overcome, rather than as a major difficulty. We share this view and have never found undue difficulty in adapting the current BS 5750 to the requirements of companies in the service sector despite its manufacturing origin.

That is not to say that separate provision for 'service' in the 1996 reissue of BS 5750 would be unwelcome but in the interim we believe there to be sufficient common ground between the quality system requirements of companies in the manufacturing and service sectors to enable BS 5750 to serve the needs of both effectively. Requirements common to both sectors include:
– the activities of both manufacturing and service companies are definable by a documented quality standard
– despite aforementioned difficulties, BS 5750 has proved a suitable documented quality standard for both, despite its later adoption by the service sector
– companies in both sectors are subject to external auditing and appraisal by customers and have to meet equivalent standards of service to continue to satisfy the needs of those customers
– both have to compete in the market for business in very similar fashion. This is particularly true since compulsory competitive tendering (CCT) was introduced to local government in the UK in the late 1980s, introducing a more commercial atmosphere to those services
– as a consequence of CCT, local government service departments began to reshape their management structure to industrial models, thereby narrowing the gap between the management styles of companies in the manufacturing and service sectors
– progressive privatisation of nationalised services reinforced that trend
– the trend was also accentuated by partial or total secession of some organisations such as schools, colleges and dental practices from direct local or government control to enable them to operate in the mode of private companies, responsive to market forces
– some companies combine manufacturing and service provision and are controlled by a common quality system
– it is a mistake to regard the service sector as a homogeneous entity, with all companies affording the same nature of service. The operations of a supermarket are quite different from those of a surgery. A local government department controlling parks and

recreation is quite different from a solicitor's practice. Differences between the activities of dissimilar companies in the service sector are probably as marked as those between any service sector company and any manufacturing company selected at random
– most clauses of BS 5750 are applicable to both manufacturers and service companies irrespective of their field of operation. For example the clauses of BS 5750, Part 2 listed in Table 5 would certainly have to be addressed in the documented quality system of all companies in both the manufacturing and service sectors. Those clauses not listed might not be applicable to certain companies in either sector, in which case a brief explanatory statement in their Master Quality Manual would suffice.

For example a service such as a surgery might not require a procedure for Clause 4.11 Inspection and test status or for Clause 4.14 Handling, storage, packaging and delivery. A manufacturer of hand-woven goods for the tourist trade might not need procedures for 4.6 Purchaser supplied product or 4.10 Inspection, measuring and test equipment. Both companies however could well need to address all the clauses of Table 5 to the requirements of the Standard.

Table 5 List of clauses of BS 5750, Part 2 common to most manufacturing and service companies, irrespective of operation
4.1 Management responsibility
4.2 Quality system
4.3 Contract review
4.4 Document control
4.5 Purchasing
4.7 Product identification and traceabililty
4.8 Process control (to be interpreted as service control by those in the service sector)
4.9 Inspection and testing
4.12 Control of nonconforming product (service in the case of service companies)
4.13 Corrective action
4.15 Quality records
4.16 Internal quality audits
4.17 Training

Thus there is much common ground between the requirements of the documented quality systems of companies in the manufacturing and service sectors.

12.2 Differences between the manufacturing and service industries

Having suggested that there is common ground between the quality requirements of companies in the manufacturing and service sectors, we do not now intend to propose the opposite. There are however some obvious differences and in this section we examine their impact on two important clauses of BS 5750, Part 1, 4.4 Design control and 4.10 Inspection and testing.

By doing so we wanted to establish whether such differences were critical, making it impossible or very difficult for BS 5750 to accommodate and address them properly, or minor, presenting no major problem in accommodating the requirements of companies in both the manufacturing and service sectors to BS 5750.

Clause 4.4: Design control

Designing a product follows a controlled sequence, with verification at various stages that output conforms to the design plan. A typical product design sequence was reviewed in Chapter 11. Design of a service is intended to conform to a similar procedure by meeting the identical requirements of Clause 4.4, Design control, of BS 5750, Part 1.

To show that there is no difficulty in principle in addressing service design via the current BS 5750, Part 1, we give below the statement we make on design in our own Master Quality Manual for delivery of consultancy service.

Procedures shall be maintained to ensure that design control is introduced at the outset of all our consultancy projects and reviewed at all appropriate stages with the client.

Design control shall be applied to all relevant aspects of our client relationships, in particular:
– planning and design of consultancy projects, including drawing up of action plans and terms of reference defining each stage of the overall project
– planning and design of specific technical inputs to client contracts e.g. product, process and plant developments undertaken on behalf of the clients, whether as part of an overall consultancy provision or as separately negotiated assignments
– at all appropriate stages the client shall be brought into design control and review and previous design proposals and provisions shall be amended to mutual acceptance as appropriate
– design outputs shall be recorded by the consultancy and verified by trial as appropriate

– design changes shall be recorded after verification of their reliability and their suitability to the client.

Far from finding BS 5750, Part 1 incompatible with the delivery of our service we found it helped to focus it by demanding formal verification of achievement at relevant stages by both parties, that is supplier (the consultancy) and purchaser (the client).

Clause 4.10:   Inspection and testing

Manufacturers make product. Service companies provide a service. You can walk round a pallet of the manufacturer's product, touch it, inspect it and verify that it is labelled correctly and that it is safely built. You cannot walk round a pallet of an airline's service or a college of education's delivery of a course. Does this mean that an airline or college are unable to verify the effectiveness of their service?

Not so. Airline service can be verified in a variety of ways such as by analysis of flight punctuality records, safety records and perceived or assessed passenger comfort. College courses are subject to external and internal inspection, auditing and monitoring by processes not unlike those used by assessing bodies to BS 5750 on their clients.

Admittedly, operating procedures describing verification in the three different situations, manufacturer, airline and college would be quite unlike each other. The least readily quantifiable might be the college output but that does not mean that it is not quantifiable. A college's self-verification procedure might well be more complex than that of a manufacturer by being based on subjective as well as objective data. Subjective factors might include, for example, students' perceptions of the efficiency of lecturing and of the relevance of courses to their career needs. Objective factors would be likely to include pass rates compared with those of other relevant colleges, average marks and gradings achieved.

The fact that subjective judgement may feature prominently in inspection and verification procedures used by companies in the service sector does not detract from the value of the procedures. It should also be noted that subjective judgement is not exclusive to service companies. It can play a part in product assessment too, such as:

– the use of taste panels by food processors
– hand and eye appraisal of engineering assemblies, however accurately machined and measured the components may have been.

12.3   Adaptation of BS 5750 to the service industries

The sampling exercise of Section 12.2. based upon Clauses 4.4 and 4.10 of BS 5750 indicated no major problem in addressing service as well as manufacture by means of BS 5750: 1987. This chapter concludes with a review of the Standard as applied to the Documented Quality System, as described in Chapter 3, of representative companies in the service sector.

12.3.1   A Master Quality Manual for companies in the service sector

In our experience the manual of a company in the service sector can follow the format of the manufacturing one given in Appendix 1, except for changes in wording to bring out the service aspects whenever relevant. There no question of developing a particular style of manual exclusive to service companies.

Because of their generic nature, we would expect the undernoted pages of the specimen manual of Appendix 1 to transfer to that of a service company with only slight alteration.

Generic pages of the manual needing only minor adaptation to individual circumstances are:
– title page; contents page; pages 3, 4, 5, 7, 9, 11, 17, 18, 20, 21, 22.

We would expect the pages set out below to need considerable adaptation to express the particular activities of service companies and manufacturing companies (other than Foodpro).

Non-generic pages of the manual:
– 1, 2, 6, 8, 10, 12, 13, 14, 15, 16, 17, 19, 23.

Adaptation of the non-generic pages should be considered on the following lines.

Page   1 Write a brief company profile outlining the service(s) you provide.

Page   2 State your company policy in one or two short paragraphs.

Page   6 Outline your arrangements for verification resources and personnel which will probably be entirely different from those of Foodpro. The paragraphs about the management representative and management review should need little alteration.

Page   8 Bring out the particular features controlling contract review in your service company which may be different from those of a manufacturer. Few dental surgeons for example proceed on the basis of written contracts with their clients and their manual and procedures should make this clear.

Page 10 Depending on the service provided, the purchasing procedure of a service company may be less concerned with materials (of which they may use few) than with the specialist people they employ or retain on a part time consultative basis. This situation applies to consultancies and legal practices whose main purchases may be the expert practitioners they employ, although they should not overlook control of their main office materials. Other service companies such as car maintenance firms, dentists and doctors may be heavily involved in the purchase of materials used in their work, in which case they could follow the general lines of page 10.

Page 12 Minor adaptation of the tone of page 12, Appendix 1, may be necessary to bring out the service aspect, especially if advice is provided to clients in the form of written reports. Traceability control of reports might be addressed on the following lines.
– 'All work in progress and finished reports on client projects, whether on computer software or hard copy, shall be identifiable to the client and the project and shall be correctly stored and maintained.'
Traceability requirements within the client's business should not be forgotten and in a consultancy service could well be addressed on the following lines.
– 'The latest product identification and traceability requirements of clients' industries shall be studied and introduced to clients' quality assurance systems within our consultancy provision.

Page 13 Process control as in Clause 4.9 of BS 5750, Part 2 should clearly be interpreted as service control and addressed accordingly. As the service may be anything from provision of legal advice to stripping and servicing a car engine it is obvious that this section requires an exact statement of the service provided. Section 12.3.2 has more to say on service control.

Page 14 As discussed on page 131, methods used by service sector companies for verifying conformity of their output to customer requirement may differ from those of manufacturers. This aspect should be studied by service companies and expressed in their own terms.

Page 15 The requirement for control of test and measuring equipment might not arise in certain service provisions, for example, in solicitors' practices but where it does, it should be addressed on lines given on page 15 of the draft manual of Appendix 1. Obvious examples of service companies requiring tight controls for this clause, because they use critical equipment, are dental surgeries; hospitals; general medical practices and vehicle maintenance firms.

Page 16 Again, marking of 'inspection and test status' requires a response in the quality manual which is fully descriptive of the service provided. If the service is not product centred but concerned with provision of expertise such as consultancy, an appropriate statement might, depending on circumstances, take the form.

'Our product consists of the under listed material provided to clients as part or all of a project undertaken on their behalf:

– drawings; calculations; terms of reference for projects; action plans; interim reports; final reports; addenda to reports; written expert advice; new or modified products or devices; computer disks containing some or all of the foregoing

– all such product shall be clearly identified to its purpose and status and the authority for its issue to clients clearly marked on it or otherwise identified.'

Page 17 Statements on control of nonconforming product by a service sector company may require a different emphasis from those of a manufacturer because they may not be concerned with immediately available, tangible product. Companies providing expertise only may consider tackling it as set out below or similar lines.

'Nonconforming data provided by us, such as erroneous calculations or reports, shall be recovered from clients at no cost to them immediately the error is discovered and replaced with emended material. Software held by us and containing the error shall be wiped clean or scrapped and the client recommended to do the same or return affected disks to us.

As soon as full remedial action has been taken through corrective action procedures, emended versions shall be provided to the client.'

Page 19 Arrangements for handling, storage, packaging and delivery of product and service are very specific to individual companies who should therefore summarise their own particular arrangements in this page of the manual.

In companies providing consultancy and related services these may be very simple, for example, they may only need to wrap product such as a report in a stout envelope and post it to the client. Nevertheless their manual statement should make a clear statement on that simple operation. If special protection is needed for a report or computer disk in transit, such as padded envelopes or packages, this should be stated. So too should any special postal requirements such as insurance, recorded delivery or door to door delivery.

Page 23 Some service companies might use, or provide to clients, statistical services of a different nature from those of a manufacturer, such as market research surveys, opinion polls and the like. If so they should list them in their manual.

12.3.2   Operating procedures for companies in the service sector

Chapter 3 listed what we consider to be the generic clauses of BS 5750, Part 2, applying to all firms in a similar format. These are listed below.

4.1   Management responsibility
4.2   Quality system
4.4   Document control
4.7   Product identification and iraceability
4.12 Control of nonconforming product
4.13 Corrective action
4.15 Quality records
4.16 Internal quality qudits
4.17 Training

Chapters 4 to 7 then provided detailed guidance notes on how to prepare operating procedures for them.

We recommend that companies in the service sector adopt these procedures for use in their own situations. They should not need to alter them except for possible rewording of some parts of procedures 4.7 and 4.12 to reflect their particular service requirements more clearly.

Procedures for the non-generic clauses are another matter as they must describe the practices within specific companies. In our view the clause which most clearly brings out the personality of a company is the one defining process control. This should be addressed by means of clear operating procedures, work instructions and quality records and you are on the way to defining the nature and essence of a company.

Chapter 3 provided a proposed list of operating procedures for a large manufacturing company (a dairy). Chapter 9 listed those suitable for process control of a contrasting situation – a small company from the service sector (a carpet laying firm). In both instances the procedures defining process control reflected the markedly different provisions of each.

This chapter on the service sector concludes by proposing operating procedures to define process control in five quite different types of service company. The lists of procedures are intended to indicate general lines of approach to service control in these companies rather than total definition of their needs, which clearly could vary from company to company. The first list is for the carpet laying company previously discussed. The remainder are for four other service companies of quite different styles.

For convenience all the procedures are prefixed by the figure 9 to correspond to Clause 4.9 of BS 5750, Part 1 even if not all the companies concerned would necessarily seek registration to Part 1 as opposed to Part 2 of BS 5750.

Suggested Process Control Procedures for a small carpet laying company

Procedure 9.1: Principles of flooring installation
Procedure 9.2: Toolkit maintenance
Procedure 9.3: Floor preparation
Procedure 9.4: Installation of sheet and tile flooring
Procedure 9.5: Installation of textile floor coverings
Procedure 9.6: Installation of carpet tiles

These six short procedures each of two or three pages doubled as work instructions and defined the company's total service pro-vision.

Suggested Process Control Procedures for a swimming pool

Procedure 9.1: Reception operation and control
Procedure 9.2: Shift planning
Procedure 9.3: Swimming pool operation and control
Procedure 9.4: Ancillary plant operation and control
Procedure 9.5: Changing room and toilets: operation and control
Procedure 9.6: Refuse collection
Procedure 9.7: Cleaning operation and control

Suggested Process Control Procedures for a training agency

Procedure 9.1: Training policy and overview of system
Procedure 9.2: Course organisation and provision
Procedure 9.3: Seminar organisation and provision
Procedure 9.4: Visual aids: operation and control
Procedure 9.5: Marking and grading of trainees
Procedure 9.6: Certification of trainees

Suggested Process Control Procedures for a dental surgery

Procedure 9.1: Patient reception
Procedure 9.2: Technician support: in-house
Procedure 9.3: Technician support: external
Procedure 9.4: Instruments: operation and control
Procedure 9.5: General purpose dental materials: operation and control
Procedure 9.6: Controlled drugs: operation and control
Procedure 9,7: Delivery of dental surgery: operation and control
Procedure 9.8: Patient after care

Suggested Process Control Procedures for a car sales service

Procedure 9.1: Customer contact
Procedure 9.2: Describing and demonstrating the product
Procedure 9.3: Finance and related
Procedure 9.4: Concluding a sale
Procedure 9.5: Handing over the new car
Procedure 9.6: After sales service

From a study of these lists of outline process/service control operating procedures for a number of service companies of quite different types, it should be apparent that BS 5750: 1987 can effectively address service as well as product through Clause 4.9 of BS 5750, Part 1.

As the rest of the comparison between manufacture and service in this chapter has failed to uncover any major difficulty in either case in adapting to BS 5750, we conclude that the Standard, in its 1987 version, can serve the quality requirements of both sectors.

Part 4 – BS 5750/ISO 9000: Assessment and Beyond

Preparing for assessment

Contents of chapter:

13.1 Assessment bodies for BS 5750

In order to carry out 'third party assessment' of companies' quality systems (such as BS 5750) an aspiring 'Third Party Assessment and Certification Body' must first submit itself to scrutiny by the government sponsored National Accreditation Council for Certification Bodies (NACCB). The applicant company is required to prove its competence to the NACCB by carrying out a number of third party assessments of suppliers' quality management systems.

During the 1980s there were only a handful of accredited assessment bodies, of which the largest was (and is at the time of writing) British Standards Institute Quality Assurance (BSiQA). In the late 1980s and early 1990s several factors encouraged others to enter the field.

– The British Ministry of Defence decided to replace direct approval of contractors by third party accreditation of the contractors' quality systems to international standards.

– This had a knock on effect to subcontractors.

– The 'third party assessment' concept spread to other sectors, for example, many purchasers outside defence saw an opportunity to place the responsibility for auditing suppliers to the suppliers themselves by asking them to proceed to BS 5750 or similar third party assessed quality systems.

– Some made registration to, for example, BS 5750 within a reasonable time scale a condition of remaining on their buyers' lists. (Some were later to realise that third party assessment of a supplier's quality management system was not always achieving the same aims as product and process conformity audits carried out by themselves or consultants working for them. Nevertheless they continued to perceive third party assessment of their suppliers' overall quality systems as a bonus).

– There was unexpectedly rapid uptake of BS 5750 by service companies, some of which, such as local council service departments, were obliged by their Boards to achieve registration to it to enhance their tendering capability.

– Some central purchasing organisations such as the British National Health Procurement Directorate began to place similar constraints on their suppliers. The qualifying quality system for continuing supply to such organisations was frequently BS 5750 or a close approximation to it, adapted to their individual requirements.

These factors expanded the scope for third party assessors. New entrants to the field began to achieve accreditation as assessing bodies by NACCB and to tender their services in competition with the previously established ones. Whereas there were only six accredited assessment companies in the UK in 1987 the number had risen to twenty five by 1993.

Some are specialist in scope, mainly serving companies in a particular industrial or service sector, as denoted by company names such as:

– Steel Construction QA Scheme Ltd
– Water Industry Certification Scheme
– British Approvals Service for Electric Cables
– Ceramic Industry Certification Scheme.

Others such as BSiQA and Lloyds QA have the resources to assess companies in most manufacturing and service sectors.

The full current list of Third Party Assessment and Certification Bodies is available from the NACCB at:

19 Buckingham Gate
London SW1E 6LB.

We are not in a position to offer a critique of the relative merits of these bodies, nor would it be appropriate to do so. Some generalisations are however in order.

1 The assessment fees charged by small assessment bodies are generally lower than those of national scale companies.

2 If a small assessment body has satisfied NACCB by passing all the required tests, its ability to assess to BS 5750 and related systems should not be open to doubt. A certificate conferred by it should be of equivalent status to those issued by the larger companies.

3 On the other hand a certificate awarded by a small assessment company may not always appear to some companies to have the same prestige as one awarded by the market leader. This purely subjective judgement can be an important consideration for some companies when selecting an assessment company.

4 All assessing bodies carry out continuing surveillance of the quality systems of registered companies (and of course charge for it). Some also carry out a complete reassessment of their clients' quality systems against BS 5750 from scratch at regular intervals e.g. every three years. Others operate on the basis of continuing surveillance without a periodic total reassessment against BS 5750.

5 Some companies prefer to be assessed to BS 5750 by a body with technical expertise in its own specialised sphere of operation such as steelmaking, ceramics or water control. They may expect such an assessment to be more practical and beneficial than one by a body which covers the whole spectrum of trade and industry.

6 Some assessing bodies have a faster response than others to requests for visits, quotations for assessment and arrangement of assessment dates.

7 Some have a better initial provision of service and advice to potential clients than others. BSiQA for example offer a free preliminary visit by an appropriately qualified person to potential clients to go into matters with them and advise them on their quality system should they wish.

13.2   When and how to apply to the assessing body of your choice

13.2.1   When to apply

All assessing bodies have to plan their assessments well in advance. Many have a waiting list of clients for assessment, particularly in industries where there is rapid uptake of BS 5750. Depending on circumstances, the delay between application for assessment and actual assessment can vary from one to as many as five or six months. Generally, the larger an assessing body, the more likely is it to be prone to delay between application and assessment because of the scale of their operation.

Therefore companies aiming for registration should consider applying to their assessing body some five to six months before their intended assessment date. A delay of up to six months from application is not normally an embarrassment to most applicant companies as the time can be profitably used to run in their quality system.

If market or other forces impel them to an earlier assessment they should find assessing bodies sympathetic to a request for priority treatment. Even the busiest ones can generally rearrange their schedules to fit in a genuinely urgent case within two or three months.

As mentioned in Chapter 2, Getting started, companies developing their quality systems to BS 5750 from scratch particularly rapidly, say over six months, should allow for possible assessment backlogs by applying to their assessing body at the outset of their programme.

13.2.2 How to apply

Assessment bodies are required to assess all relevant locations of client companies. For example a company with three factories, to one of which is annexed the company head office, will require a separate charged assessment of all three locations. Typically such companies proceed to registration on a site by site basis over a period of time with one of them acting as pathfinder for the group. The remaining two locations can then profit from the experience of the pathfinder and can generally make rapid progress to registration.

If all three were to reach assessment readiness simultaneously, most assessment bodies would respond appropriately by carrying out assessment of all the group locations at or around the same time. In that situation the total group assessment fee might well less than the total of three separate assessments spread over a period of time.

Application to a listed assessment body for a quotation for assessment to BS 5750 is a simple matter of lifting the telephone and announcing your requirement. Typically you will be sent a description of the assessing company and an outline of its approach to assessing companies to BS 5750. There will also be a questionnaire asking for details of your company, the location(s) to be assessed and your intended scope of registration as described in Chapter 2.

The methods of assessing companies differ in points of detail from this stage. If the questionnaire is sufficiently definitive and the reply to it clear and uncomplicated, this may enable some to prepare a quotation for assessment and to offer a choice of dates. If there are complications an initial meeting at the targeted location to iron out details may be needed before a quotation can be provided.

Assessing bodies will then send for and scrutinise the Documented Quality System of the client company to assess its conformity with BS 5750. Some require the whole DQS (as described in Chapter 3) to be sent whereas others will ask for only the Master Quality Manual and an outline of the remainder of the documented system. In both cases, if there are deficiencies these will be pointed out to the client company who will be asked to put them right.

Some assessing bodies will then, as a matter of routine, visit the targeted location to examine the operation of the documented system as a form of limited assessment before the official one to BS 5750. Others offer this preliminary limited assessment as an option, enabling the client, should they prefer, to proceed direct to assessment on the strength of confirmation of their DQS at the assessment company's office.

Preliminary assessment has the advantage of affording a company improved prospects of immediate registration after full assessment to BS 5750 but it costs more. It is particularly popular with companies whose peers in the Group have already achieved registration to BS 5750 and who want to keep up the Group record. It would also enhance the prospects of companies under pressure from customers to achieve registration soon.

13.3   A model 'Eve of Assessment' self-check routine to trap last minute errors

A company undergoing assessment to BS 5750 has to demonstrate two things to the satisfaction of the assessment body.
1 That it has a documented quality system which accurately describes its operations in compliance with BS 5750.
2 That the company's practices are as defined by their documented system when audited on location by the assessors.

Chapter 2 provided a Model Action Plan for BS 5750: from development to assessment. If effectively implemented in the months leading to assessment, both the above aims will have been met by the time eve of assessment is reached. There should therefore be no need for special checks on the eve of assessment.

That is to ignore Murphy's Law which states that anything that can go wrong will do so on the date(s) of assessment. The following eve of assessment checklist is based on that premise. We recommend that you put it into operation (or a variant adapted to your own requirements) on the day before assessment.

We have never applied it without being thankful that we did so, because even the most prepared of firms have been surprised to find how many matters there were to put right on the eve of assessment. They were invariably pleased that they had carried out the self-check routine when the actual assessment took place. The whole tone of the place had been improved the day before.

We believe that 'on the eve', that is the day before, assessment is right. The certain knowledge of assessment the next day concentrates the mind. It is simply not the same if done a week earlier.

Eve of assessment checks: manufacturing companies

1 Does *everybody* know the assessment starts tomorrow?
2 Does everyone know his/her job?
3 Well enough to answer questions on it if asked by an assessor?
4 Are any key employees expected to be away from the factory during assessment?
5 If so, is there effective cover through deputies?
6 Do the deputies have access to all relevant documents handled by the absent boss?
7 Do they need any last minute refreshers on them or on other matters normally controlled by their boss?
8 Are all processes under effective control?
9 Are they all identified by batch numbers and so on if appropriate?
10 Is such marking immediately obvious to a visiting assessor? If in doubt, go over the top a little. Consider placing activity markers by processes if relevant, for example, immediately by each major activity position a clipboard or equivalent giving: Product/Process: Batch Number: Quality Records (attach).
11 Are instruments marked with 'calibration' or 'not under calibration' labels or are there suitable alternative arrangements?
12 Are quarantined goods (if any) clearly marked and segregated?
13 Is each parcel of quarantined goods separated from its neighbours and identified with 'hold notes'? (Consider collating each parcel, for example, by stretch wrapping.)
14 Does each quarantined parcel trace to a register by means of a unique number on the 'hold note'?
15 Are all raw materials and products clearly labelled and marked with a goods received number, batch number, or equivalent as appropriate?
   (Replace *all* missing labels and markers. It will pay dividends tomorrow.)
16.1 Are all training records up to date?
16.2 And filed for immediate reference?
17 Are all quality records up to date? (For example, for purchasing, internal quality auditing, corrective actions.)
18 Are they filed for immediate reference? (Delegate this to the

Document Controller or equivalent who should spend all of today chasing this and plugging last minute gaps.)

19 Are the factory and precincts neat and tidy? BS 5750, Part 2 is not primarily a GMP assessment but a neat and tidy area inspires confidence. Carry out a full *Good Housekeeping* drive. Dispose of all surplus and waste material *today*, including old documents, redundant labels into a skip or skips which should leave the factory tonight. Ensure all toilets are clean and fully provided with the necessary facilities.

20 Have any jobs or processes crept in recently which are not recorded in your Scope of Registration? If so, discuss them with your assessor.

The assessment and after

Contents of chapter:

14.1 How assessors operate

Assessors to BS 5750 are people well experienced in industry or commerce, typically with a background in quality assurance or related functions, who have decided to specialise wholly or partly in assessment of quality assurance systems. They may afford their services to assessment bodies on a part-time basis on secondment from their normal duties, for example, consultancy, or may be full-time employees of an assessment body.

Registration as an assessor is achieved through the IQA (Institute of Quality Assurance) who require evidence of appropriate experience and further credentials such as:
– possession of a certificate denoting successful completion of an Assessor's training course – typically a one week residential course involving practical case studies and a written examination
– evidence of recent participation in a qualifying number of quality audits to BS 5750 or equivalent systems.

A higher rung on the assessor ladder is Lead Assessor, promotion to which requires evidence of a stronger auditing record and wider experience than those applicable to assessor grade. The auditing records of both assessors and Lead Assessors need to be kept current and active for retention on a register of authorised assessors maintained by the IQA.

A Lead Assessor may be the sole assessor of a small company or location if it requires only a single assessor day to audit its compliance to BS 5750. Longer assessments may be carried out by a Lead Assessor working solo for several days or by an assessor or team of assessors working under a Lead Assessor. The Lead Assessor will communicate beforehand with the company seeking registration beforehand and inform them of the form the assessment will take and the special requirements, if any, of the assessor(s).

At the start of the first day of assessment the auditing team (assuming a team to be necessary) will request an opening meeting with the 'auditees' (representatives of the company being assessed). The Lead Assessor will introduce his team, explain their roles in the assessment and restate the aims of the assessment. The audit programme will probably have been agreed by both parties beforehand but if any alterations are necessary they can be covered at this stage.

Other details to be confirmed at the opening meeting are:
– provision of guides by the company to take the assessors to the various functions to be audited
– facilities normally requested by the assessing team such as protective clothing and access to a small office
– the method of reporting to be used by the assessors
– any restrictions which it may be necessary to impose on the assessors such as limited or barred access to hazardous processes.

The assessment should now be ready to begin.

14.2   What assessors look for during assessment

In general terms, the remit of the assessors is to seek evidence of the undernoted. More specific details are provided at the end of this section.
– Valid, up to date documented procedures and instructions which are in operation and available where required.
– Correct operation of these procedures by the appropriate people.
– Clear quality records giving evidence of current and recent conformity to the quality system.
– Clearly defined responsibilities for work done.
– Adequate personnel and resources for work done.
– Effective quality auditing and corrective action.

They assess compliance with the above by visiting all appropriate departments and auditing what they see, ideally against pre-prepared checklists detailing the points to be covered. They are fully experienced in the technique of auditing by sampling. If a sample observation (for example, whether a thermometer is under correct calibration control) reveals no discrepancy they will accept it as conforming, tick their record sheet and move on to the next point to be checked.

If a discrepancy is found it will be drawn to the attention of the auditee and noted to the assessor's record as either a minor or major nonconformance against BS 5750. Sometimes the auditee will be asked to rectify a minor nonconformance during the assessment, in which case the corrective action will be noted by the assessor and the matter closed.

At the end of the assessment (or at the end of each day if it goes beyond a day) the Lead Assessor and team will meet with the auditees and review their findings. The various possible outcomes of assessment and their implication to the auditee are discussed in Section 14.3.

As a more specific guide to the mode of operation of the assessors, listed below against clause numbers of ISO 9002, are some of the more common deficiencies found by them during auditing of manufacturing companies' quality systems to that standard. Clearly, as many of these as possible should be eliminated by auditees before assessment.

Clause 4.1: Management responsibility
Responsibility and authority for quality related work not always clearly defined or falling too heavily on one person such as the quality controller.
Management reviews not being carried out.

Clause 4.2:　Quality system
Slack implementation of some documented procedures

Clause 4.3:　Contract review
An ineffective system for 'error trapping' telephoned orders

Clause 4.4:　Document control
Unauthorised documents in operation.
Obsolete documents in operation.
No master list of documents available.
Master list available but no reference to control of externally imposed documents such as industry codes of practice.
The system for varying documents is too informal.
(It will be noted that documentary deficiencies are common. BS 5750 requires a strong documented system.)

Clause 4.5　Purchasing
No list of approved subcontractors.
Ineffective grading of subcontractors.
Poor definition of purchases on orders.

Clause 4.6　Purchaser supplied product
This is seldom a problem area in our experience.

Clause 4.7   Product identification and traceability
This is seldom a problem area. Most companies by now have effective marking and traceability arrangements where essential in their operations or demanded by contract.

Clause 4.8   Process Control
Informal monitoring and control of process variables with little or no recording.
Inadequate process specifications leaving too much to interpretation by the operators.
Poor commissioning and verification of processes and equipment.

Clause 4.9   Inspection and testing
Surprisingly free of error by and large considering the demands of this clause. Most companies take inspection seriously and provide accordingly.

Clause 4.10   Inspection, measuring and test equipment
No list of instruments under calibration.
Calibration subcontractor(s) not listed.
Calibration status of instruments not marked.
Inadequate calibration procedures.
Inadequate procedures for monitoring the fitness for purpose of instruments between calibrations.

Clause 4.11:   Inspection and test status

Poor marking of sequentially assembled items to show that they have passed interim inspections and tests (This is not always practicable with fast moving continuous processes for which inspection records should provide the necessary assurances.)

Clause 4.12:   Control of nonconforming product
Nonconforming product poorly marked and segregated.
No quarantine area available, even on a temporary basis.
No records kept of inspection after rework has been necessary.

Clause 4.13:   Corrective action
Insufficient attention to prevention of recurrence of faults once corrective action has been taken.

Clause 4.14:   Handling, storage, packaging and delivery
Inappropriate handling and storage methods risking product damage.
Inadequate continuous measurement and recording of temperature of cold stores and refrigerated vehicles.
No list of approved subcontractors.

Clause 4.15:   Quality records
Unclearly headed quality records from pre-BS 5750, Part 2 days.
Poorly filed quality records.
Retention time of quality records not stated in writing.

Clause 4.16:   Internal quality audits
The auditing system is of a kind that does not conform to BS 5750.
Audits and follow up actions have lapsed.
Audit forms and follow up actions not signed off.

Clause 4.17:   Training
Not all employees have a training record on file.
Appropriate 'quality training' has not taken place.
The training needs of people have not been formally identified and
recorded in writing.

Clause 4.18   Statistical techniques
This is not normally a problem area. Companies normally install
appropriate systems.

14.3   Assessment outcomes: unconditional pass; minor referral; major referral

Generally a company showing only minor nonconformances
during assessment will have an excellent chance of being recommended for registration. One or more major will almost certainly
result in a referral. All of this will be made clear to the auditee by the
Lead Assessor at an exit meeting.

Sometimes there can be an atmosphere at these meetings as the
auditees' perceptions of particular nonconformances may clash
with those of the assessors. Obviously if faults are on the borderline
between minor and major and their classification by the assessor as
'major' fails the company, this will be a disappointment to the
auditees. We can only counsel them to grin and bear it in these
circumstances. Lead Assessors do not lightly categorise nonconformances as major. They are not infallible but they are liable to
interpret BS 5750 more accurately than the auditees. However it is
worth recording that there is an appeal procedure whereby the
auditee can seek a reversal of an assessor's verdict should they be
particularly dissatisfied with it.

We have been involved with companies who failed on a single
major nonconformance which they themselves regarded as minor.
After their initial disappointment subsided they began to see the
rights of the assessors' case and accepted it philosophically.

On a descending scale of success, the following are the alternative outcomes of assessment.

– The assessment fails to reveal a single minor or major nonconformance or only a few minor ones which were rectified to compliance by the auditee during assessment. Outcome: recommendation for immediate registration to BS 5750.

– The assessment reveals no major nonconformances but a number of minor ones are listed which require some time to rectify. Likely outcome: the company are asked to write to the assessment company explaining how they propose to rectify the faults and, subject to a satisfactory response, will be recommended for immediate registration.

– The assessment reveals a number of minor nonconformances and one or a few major ones. Likely outcome: the company is referred for a limited reassessment. Again they will be asked to write to the assessment body outlining their action plan to rectify all the nonconformances. As the major ones are likely to take some time, the assessing body may propose a date for reassessment some months ahead. The reassessment will largely concentrate on how effectively the faults detected during assessment have been rectified and whether the revised procedures are now in compliance with BS 5750. This is by no means as bad an outcome as may seem at first. Faults have been found on audit but no serious flaws in the overall quality system have been signalled. Provided the company respond appropriately they are likely to be reassessed by the same Lead Assessor on a much more limited basis than before at a fraction of the cost. Many sound companies fall into this category and we regard this outcome as more of a success, albeit a deferred one, than a failure.

– Numerous major nonconformances are found as well as a host of minor ones. Likely outcome: the company are advised to go back to the drawing board on their BS 5750 system and rework it to compliance over a period of time. Only when this has been completed they should then contact their assessment body for a total reassessment of their system. In effect they would be treated as a brand new applicant by having their entire quality system audited. Fortunately this outcome is now relatively rare as most companies have become sufficiently well informed on BS 5750 to proceed for assessment only when they have a well developed and active system in operation.

When responding to your assessment body on remedial actions you plan to take on nonconformances, we suggest that you allocate time and effort to make a good job of your reply, stating exactly what you have done or are about to do on each. You will have been given a copy of the assessors' report before they left your premises and this will list each nonconformance clearly and individually. Use it as the basis of your reply and respond clearly to each against their reference numbers.

14.4   Upkeep and maintenance of the BS 5750 system after registration

Assessment continues after registration to ensure that registered companies maintain their quality systems to BS 5750. Typically this entails limited site reassessments at about six monthly intervals. Some assessing bodies' certification processes also require a three yearly total audit as this follows the style of certain centralised purchasing organisations.

The assessing body may agree the six monthly audits in advance with the client company and they will follow a pre-determined plan. In this way the whole quality system is monitored as part of the programme and key aspects of the business can be given priority in the scheme. Some, for example internal quality audits, management reviews and corrective actions, may be monitored at every audit as they indicate how effectively the system is operating.

Some assessing bodies are evolving to the concept of assessor as consultant to the client company rather than external invigilator. This is a praiseworthy development as it helps to reduce the element of 'them and us' on these occasions. Nevertheless assessors do have an invigilating role and the periodic audits are not to be taken lightly. In some ways they can be as searching as the original assessment and if a company seriously flouts the rules of BS 5750, it can be recommended for de-registration.

Beyond BS 5750 to Total Quality Management (TQM)

Contents of chapter:

15.1 The case for Total Quality Management or equivalent

There is widespread agreement that a company should not rest on its laurels when registration to BS 5750 has been achieved but instead should use it as the basis of a 'total' quality management programme extending to every facet of its operation.

Some of the elements of a Total Quality Management (TQM) programme are stated by its practitioners are as follows.
– Faults should be eliminated by application of a 'Right First Time' policy.
– It follows from this that the concept of 'acceptable quality level of faults'(AQL) as used in traditional Quality Control is something of a heresy in TQM as there should be zero faults if everyone is pulling their weight.
– Traditional management systems are too compartmentalised. Barriers have to be broken down between management and workers and between departments.
– Trying to control people through systems treats them like robots. Systems will only work if people make them work.
– Quality circles should be set up to create the right culture for TQM.
– The needs and expectations of targeted potential customers must be identified.
– Quality chains should be set up within companies operating TQM. Internal suppliers and customers should be identified by each person in the chain and their needs catered for.
– Management time and money must be committed over a period to make TQM work.
– Effective implementation of TQM demands a cultural and philosophic shift within a company.

– Each process in a department should be analysed by examination of its inputs and outputs. Input is said to consist of: materials, procedures, methods, information (including specifications), people, skills, knowledge, training, plant/equipment. Output consists of: products, services, information, paperwork.
– The 'needs and expectations' of customers and employees should be defined.
– Whenever a serious problem arises, action teams should be set up, bringing together the people best equipped to solve it, irrespective of rank or department.
– Improved business efficiency and effectiveness must be applied throughout the whole organisation.
– TQM moves the focus of control from outside the individual to within.
– TQM is user driven; it cannot be imposed from outside the organisation.
– Such self-management can lead to the removal of several layers of old style, hierarchical management.
– Teamwork is essential to effective implementation of TQM.

Compared with the definitive tone of BS 5750 some of these principles of TQM are rather general. In isolation none can be faulted but in aggregate they do not impress as guidelines to an average company seeking quality improvement over a reasonable time scale.

If the overall aims of TQM have been accurately described above, it is a formidable task as it requires a very high degree of commitment from top management and everyone in the business. Moreover it is often stated that companies have to work at it for a long time, perhaps four years, before significant improvements in product quality and supplier/customer relations result.

For the general run of companies, we prefer to re-interpret the T of TQM as I (for improved) for practical reasons.

It is possible for even quite small firms to make immediate progress on what we prefer to call 'Improved Quality Management' (IQM), after an BS 5750 or comparable quality management system has been installed and activated. IQM has the more limited objective of building upon an BS 5750 quality system by extending its principles to facets of an organisation not explicitly addressed by BS 5750.

The objectives of so called IQM may fall short of those achievable over a time scale of years with TQM but they are definable in concrete terms and can be achieved reasonably quickly without the philosophic shift within the company deemed necessary for TQM. Manufacturing and service companies should give

IQM serious consideration, if only as a staging post on the way to the more extended TQM.

What we mean by IQM and how to go about it are reviewed in Section 15.2.

15.2   BS 5750 as a basis for TQM or equivalent

15.2.1   What we mean by TQM or equivalent

Section 15.1 introduced the concept of IQM which explains the term 'TQM or equivalent' in the titles of Sections 15.1 and 15.2'.

To recapitulate, TQM as currently defined is a long haul for a company, even if it has gained registration to BS 5750. Companies prepared to undertake a co-ordinated drive to TQM and to allocate all the necessary resources to it over a period of time, maybe years, might well begin by acquiring a further two British Standard Specifications (described in Chapter 1) to help them plan their strategy:
– BS 7850, Parts 1 and 2, Total Quality Management
– BS 7750, Environmental Management Systems.

Between these two specifications they should have the framework for their TQM programme. From that starting point no two companies will follow exactly the same path to implement TQM, as perception of it and its implementation are so much a matter of individual company culture.

Many firms, especially the smaller independents wishing to develop their quality system beyond BS 5750, will benefit from a simpler quality improvement programme than one leading all the way to TQM. This brings us back to our so-called IQM as introduced and loosely defined in Section 15.1.

Like TQM, IQM accepts that BS 5750 registration is a basis for continuing quality improvement and not an end in itself. In contrast to the long lead time to TQM admitted by its protagonists, improvement through IQM can begin to show up quite soon on a practical level as we define it as a planned extension of BS 5750. We reason as follows.

BS 5750, Part 1 has twenty clauses, all of which must have been correctly and adequately addressed by a company to have gained registration to BS 5750, Part 1. By registration time the company will have increased its general quality awareness considerably and will have overcome any initial resistance it may have harboured to implementing a demanding documented quality system. Already therefore the 'company culture' is predisposed to 'IQM' through its regular quality audits, management reviews and process analyses.

It is now appropriate to initiate IQM by extending the principles of BS 5750, already assimilated into the company, to other facets of the organisation not so far addressed by that standard, for example:
– health and safety
– control of environmental matters
– marketing
– customer relations.

These are only four examples. Development of IQM need not stop there but can be extended into other functions as appropriate. Even financial control is worth considering. Although traditionally subject to formal control and auditing, it can be beneficial in an IQM programme to encourage accountants to become more demonstrably active in the overall company quality scheme. In the best companies this is already the case. In the worst the accountant may be a number cruncher with little overall involvement.

We believe that some companies miss an opportunity by restricting their accountants to financial control. Accountants are of course numerate but are also familiar with scrutinising and auditing procedures and could well serve not only as Management Representative to BS 5750 in certain types of company but could also play a leading part in IQM.

15.2.2   How to install and implement IQM

We suggest the following outline plan as a practical mode of progress to IQM following registration to BS 5750.

Stage 1 Identify the additional functions you wish to pull into an extended quality system beyond BS 5750.

Stage 2 Consider allocating to each a clause number beyond those of BS 5750. For the examples given above these could well be as underlisted in an BS 5750, Part 1 programme, with progress beyond 'Clause 24' for further company functions as desired.
– Clause 21: Control of health and safety
– Clause 22: Control of environmental matters
– Clause 23: Control of marketing
– Clause 24: Control of customer relations.

Stage 3 Establish what you want to achieve in these clauses beyond BS 5750 and write it down. You may wish to set out the objectives of each clause in the manner of BS 5750, leaving as little room for misinterpretation as possible.

Stage 4 Now study the application of each to the organisation and write procedures, work instructions and quality records for each just as you did for the clauses of BS 5750.

Stage 5 Implement and audit them as for BS 5750. They are now part of your extended BS 5750 system and you have made the first developments to IQM as we perceive it.

15.2.3   Procedures for IQM

This final section is concerned with suggestions about writing procedures for the undernoted four clauses identified as suitable as the start of an improved quality programme beyond BS 5750:
- Clause 21: Control of health and safety
- Clause 22: Control of environmental matters
- Clause 23: Control of marketing
- Clause 24: Control of customer relations.

Clause 21:   Control of health and safety

Some companies have very demanding health and safety obligations controlled by measures well beyond the scope of these notes. It would obviously be wholly inappropriate for North Sea oil companies or petrochemicals processors to address health and safety by means of this twenty first clause of an extended BS 5750 system. So critical an aspect of their business should have been under much tighter control from inception of their operations.

At the other extreme there are many small businesses with little or no involvement in mechanical handling or other obvious potential sources of accidents, who do not perceive a health and safety obligation and who do not therefore have written procedures controlling health and safety. This is a mistake. Health and safety legislation applies to all places of work and a written assessment of risks is required of organisations employing more than five people.

Even in the simplest operations there is a case for a 'Clause 21' procedure summarising the company's general safety policy and its arrangements for complying with regulations which came into force in 1993, such as:
- the *Manual Handling Operations Regulations*
- the *Workplace (Health, Safety and Welfare) Regulations*
- the *Personal Protective Equipment at Work Regulations*
- the *Display Screen Equipment Work Regulations*
- the *Provision and Use of Work Equipment Regulations*.

The general thrust of these regulations can be inferred from their titles and obviously apply to most companies. In small companies with simple operations, a single Clause 21' procedure might define how they met the requirements of these regulations through a series of short statements.

Companies with more complex or hazardous operations would

have to go much further by taking account of additional regulations relevant to their business. These might concern, for example:
– control of substances hazardous to health (COSHH)
– occupational exposure limits
– classification and labelling of dangerous substances in-house and in transit.

Such companies would be advised to consider drawing up a series of short procedures under Clause 21 defining their arrangements for control of each regulation of that kind in their business.

Clause 22: Control of environmental matters

Again, companies' obligations under environmental control legislation vary considerably. Many offices are largely unaffected by environmental considerations. Manufacturers such as chemical processors, tanneries and waste disposal companies are heavily affected. The operations of some service companies such as waste disposal and effluent treatment organisations are so defined by environmental matters that they might well opt to install a quality system to BS 7750 which specialises in environmental control and not BS 5750 which is of general application.

Manufacturers such as chemical processes and tanneries are much more likely to opt for BS 5750 but would clearly need procedures for environmental control as an extension of that system.

Relevant British regulations at 1993 are:
– *The Environmental Protection Act* 1990
– *The Controlled Waste Regulations* 1992.

To judge their impact on companies with an active quality system to BS 5750, consider the following two examples from our recent experience. At first sight the first has no apparent need to address 'environment' at all in an extended BS 5750 system. The second obviously has.

Example 1
A small company consisting only of an office and a small warehouse was formed to export pharmaceuticals by packing them in cartons to which were added expanded polystyrene granules as protection. That was the company's sole activity. No mess was created and there were no harmful emissions such as smoke from a boiler.

Two factors however arose that required environmental control to be addressed by them:

Following a tightening of environmental controls in Germany in 1992, their German customers could no longer accept non-biodegradable polystyrene as a package cushion. The small British company responded by buying a shredder and using shredded documents as a cushion. This was environmentally acceptable by their German customers.

Overage product began to accrue as business developed and it required responsible, supervised destruction by incineration at a very high temperature. This was arranged through a local hospital who had the necessary equipment.

The above and a few simple additional points such as baling and disposal of cardboard waste were addressed in a one page environmental control procedure under Clause 22.

Example 2
A chemical solvent blending company stocks various solvents in silos and manufactures a product by a vapour phase reaction. Before BS 5750 registration it had attended well enough to its environmental obligations but had never sat down to think its total policy through and write it down.

Adoption of IQM in the form of clauses beyond Clause 20 of BS 5750, Part 1 enabled it to define its policy on environmental control more clearly and to support it with procedures detailing their arrangements. Some had been in existence before their IQM drive and were reviewed and updated. New procedures defining training, resourcing and review were written to improve the company's control of environmental affairs. That is the essence of self improvement through IQM. The procedures were for:
– capture of solvent leakages from tankers and silos (including potential accidental discharge of an entire tanker or silo load)
– scrubbing of waste gases from their reaction plant
– monitoring of air purity by instruments
– security and safety in transit of bulk tanker loads
– training of personnel in environmental control
– review of resourcing and management of environmental control.

Thus their environmental provision was appreciably in advance of that of the small company of Example 1 and was adequately addressed through IQM within a few months.

Clause 23:   Control of marketing

As a key company function, often funded by a sizeable budget, marketing is a prime candidate for inclusion in a quality improvement programme beyond BS 5750. Not to have marketing at the core of a company, in close contact with R & D, production and finance in a quality framework, would be to miss an opportunity. Marketing people have energy and imagination and see the customers' needs as closely as anyone in the organisation. They can introduce drive and enthusiasm to a company quality programme and can themselves benefit from adopting some of the controls and procedures of a quality system in their own affairs.

To take the example of developing and launching a new product the following come into the reckoning and could benefit from expression as written procedures as for contract, purchasing and process control:
– market research
– advertising
– product launch
– budget control.

Clause 24:   Control of customer relations

An extended quality programme should not only attend to the major functions such as marketing, finance and environmental control. It should also get the smaller but no less important details right. Practically every week we encounter companies whose telephone answering technique is well below standard. They take over a minute to answer and then fail to monitor whether we are connected to the right person. This would not impress a buyer wanting to place a first order with that company. If ever there was a deserving candidate for a 'Get it right first time' policy it would be telephone answering.

This and other customer relations procedures should be defined in an IQM programme and properly resourced. To stay with the example of the telephone, this simply means that resourcing should ensure that an appropriate person must always be available to answer the phone, preferably before the fifth ring.

Suggested procedures for control of customer relations are:
– define who are our customers
– face to face customer contact
– control of the telephone
– telephone sales and order processing
– customers contact by letter and fax.

We believe that Improved Quality Management as introduced and described in this section has been shown to be a valuable resource for companies wishing to extend their overall quality commitment beyond BS 5750 within a limited budget and over a realistic time scale.

By examining facets of their operation not addressed by the current versions of BS 5750, by writing clear procedures for them and by providing the resources and teamwork to implement them, it should enable companies to take a decisive step along the TQM path.

If subsequently implementing a full TQM programme, we believe that they would benefit from the IQM work already carried out.

Appendix 1

Draft Master Quality Manual to BS 5750, Part 2/ISO 9002

The following draft Master Quality Manual to BS 5750, Part 2 is for a notional food processing company called Foodpro Ltd. Foodpro Ltd is an amalgam of several food processing companies we have helped to BS 5750, Part 2. The manual is valid by addressing the notional company's operations in conformance with BS 5750, Part 2.

As much the same manual format was used for each of the food processing companies we assisted and each was duly registered to BS 5750, Part 2, we can confidently recommend adoption of the format of the manual to readers heading for BS 5750, Part 2. We have deliberately kept it concise, with only 23 pages, to show that a master quality manual need not run to great length nor need it be over formalised to conform with BS 5750, Part 2. It tells the essential facts about the business and gives away no company secrets.

Some companies provide more extensive job descriptions than those in page 5 of our draft manual and may have more elegant page heading and cross referencing systems than ours. We reiterate that the format of our draft manual can readily be adapted to individual requirements.

Amendment of the draft manual to BS 5750, Part 1 would entail renumbering the clauses in terms of BS 5750, Part 1 and supplying statements for Clauses 4.4 and 4.19 of BS 5750, Part 1.

Amendment of the manual to service companies should follow the guidelines given in Chapter 12, page 132.

Foodpro Limited
Quality Manual to BS 5750: 1987, Part 2

Prepared by:
Approved by:
Issue date:
Manual number:

Note: unauthorised amendments invalidate this manual.

This copy is controlled/uncontrolled.
(Inappropriate statement deleted by:.....................................
Date:...
Authority:...

Foodpro Ltd Quality Manual

Contents

Quality Manual

Page 1 of 23 pages
Issue number of page: First   Date of issue: 1.2.93
Date of reissue: N/A   Authority for issue:
For reason for reissue see Amendment record, Section 3.3

---

1   Company profile

Foodpro Limited were formed in 1947 as an independent family firm to produce bread and sugar confectionery for local distribution within L and district. During the 1950s and 1960s business developed to the extent that distribution became national and by 1970 the payroll had increased from an original four to thirty five.

During the 1970s the product range was widened by introduction of chilled and frozen gateaux. These began to sell into several High Street retailers and by 1988 the increased scale of operation necessitated building of new customised premises from which we continue to operate. At 1993 our total number of employees is 80.

Our plant and operating methods are appropriate to our product style and include:
– Flour and sugar storage silos to which bulk tanker loads are blown and from which metered batch quantities are automatically dispensed
– Z blade batch mixers
– Automatic dough sheeting plant
– Rotary moulders and wire cutters
– Travelling ovens
– Semi-automatic wrapping machinery
– Continuous chilling and freezing plant
– Chilled and frozen food stores

All our products are distributed by approved haulage subcontractors with appropriate refrigerated transport.

Quality Manual

Page 2 of 23 pages
Issue number of page: First   Date of issue: 1.2.93
Date of reissue: N/A   Authority for issue:
For reason for reissue see Amendment record, Section 3.3

---

2   Company quality policy

Foodpro Ltd are committed to the establishment and maintenance
of quality assurance systems, staff and equipment to ensure that
the prescribed standards of our customers are fully and consistently
met.

Our quality assurance procedures are defined by BS 5750: 1987,
Part 2 and meet the Food Safety and Good Manufacturing Practice
requirements of related documents specific to the food industry, for
example, *Food and Drink Manufacture – Good Manufacturing Practice:
A Guide to its Responsible Management*, IFST, 1991 and *Quality Systems
for the Food and Drink Industries*, Leatherhead Food RA, 1989 and as
revised.

Adoption of the systems and procedures in this manual and
appendices to it is mandatory within the company.

Quality Manual

Page 3 of 23 pages
Issue number of page: First   Date of issue: 1.2.93
Date of reissue: N/A   Authority for issue:
For reason for reissue see Amendment record, Section 3.3

3.1:   Distribution of Quality Manual

This Quality Manual is distributed in two categories: controlled and uncontrolled. Both are identical at the time and date of issue.

1 Controlled copies are given a control number and are systematically kept up to date by the issue of amendments. These copies are issued to our assessing body to BS 5750, Part 2 and to the undernoted company managers.
2 Uncontrolled copies are not numbered. They may be passed to customers on request, subject to commercial considerations. They are not covered by the amendment/updating system.

   Distribution and maintenance of the controlled copies is the responsibility of the Management Representative as defined in BS 5750.

Controlled Issue Log:

Issue No.

Date:
Manual title:

Quality Manual of Foodpro Limited

Copy No.	Manual holder	Date of issue Held by nominee	Signature
1	Chairman		
2	Managing Director		
3	Production Director		
4	Quality Manager		
5	Assessors to BS 5750, Part 2		

Quality Manual

Page 4 of 23 pages
Issue number of page: First   Date of issue: 1.2.93
Date of reissue: N/A   Authority for issue:
For reason for reissue see Amendment record, Section 3.3

3.2   Maintenance of Quality Manual

The Document Controller incorporates any new or amended documents in all manuals under his/her control as soon as they have been authorised by the Management Representative for BS 5750, or, by delegation, the Deputy.

Superseded pages are withdrawn from circulation, marked SUPERSEDED and held for at least two years for possible reference.

The new pages are marked with their new issue status and the reason for each new issue is noted on the Amendment record of Section 3.3.

3.3   Amendment record of Quality Manual

Issue number of Quality Manual: First
Date of latest authorised issue: 1.2.93
Note: eight amendments as below are allowed, after which the manual is withdrawn and reissued.

Section of manual   Title   Amendment summary   Date issued

Quality Manual

Page 5 of 23 pages
Issue number of page: First   Date of issue: 1.2.93
Date of reissue: N/A   Authority for issue:
For reason for reissue see Amendment record, Section 3.3

4.1   Management responsibility

4.1.1   Quality policy
          This is defined in Section 2 of the manual.
4.1.2   Organisation
          The company's Management Organisational System is
          indicated below with outline job descriptions of each
          manager.
4.1.2.1   Responsibility and authority of personnel affecting quality

          Managing
          Director: Responsible for overall control of company, its
          positioning in the market, its overall profitability and its
          external relations.

          Quality
          Assurance Manager: Responsible for origination, develop-
          ment and maintenance of the company's quality assurance
          system. Is the company's Management Representative for
          BS 5750.

          Production
          Director: Responsible, through a team of supervisors, for
          achievement of production targets within budgeted
          guidelines and in conformance with specified quality para-
          meters. Is the company's Deputy Management Repre-
          sentative for BS 5750.

          Quality
          Controller: Responsible for monitoring and quality
          assurance of raw materials, processes and finished product
          to prescribed procedures.

          **(Consider the validity of the above and the quality respon-
          sibilities of other managers and supervisors in your
          organisation.)**

Quality Manual

Page 6 of 23 pages
Issue number of page: First   Date of issue: 1.2.93
Date of reissue: N/A   Authority for issue:
For reason for reissue see Amendment record, Section 3.3

Management responsibility

4.1.2.2 Verification resources and personnel
   The company has two control laboratories on site. The first is devoted to rapid testing and recording of incoming raw materials. The second is concerned with process and finished product verification. Both are under the control of the Quality Controller assisted by four technical assistants fully trained in company laboratory control procedures.
   Laboratory resources comprise: (List the main items of equipment.)
   All personnel are fully trained and are encouraged to control the quality of their own work even though it is subject to formal quality inspection.

4.1.2.3 Management representative
   The company's Management Representative with special responsibility for implementing and maintaining BS 5750 is the QA Manager.
   The Deputy Management Representative is the Production Director.

4.1.3   Management review

4.1.3.1 To ensure the continuing effectiveness of the Quality System, a senior management team holds a recorded Management Review not less frequently than twice a year.

4.1.3.2 The reviews are chaired and the minutes signed by the Chairman, or by delegation, the Managing Director.

4.1.3.3 The Management Review includes the results of internal quality audits, nonconformities, corrective action, consumer complaints and the action taken to prevent recurrence of faults.

Quality Manual

Page 7 of 23 pages
Issue number of page: First   Date of issue: 1.2.93
Date of reissue: N/A   Authority for issue:
For reason for reissue see Amendment record, Section 3.3

4.2   Quality system

4.2.1 Our quality system is fully defined in this Master Manual which states that our documentation system conforms to BS 5750: 1987, Part 2.

4.2.2 Conformance to the system is mandatory unless improved. Procedures shall be officially changed after they have been agreed with the relevant people.

4.2.3 This Master Manual is a controlled document and each copy is identified against its authorised keeper. The manual is updated as required and copies of affected sheets are sent to all authorised keepers. It is their responsibility to keep a current manual. The reasons for and details of change are notified to each keeper and a master record is maintained by QA department. No photocopies of the Master Manual are recognised.

4.2.4 If the manual is amended, the index page is updated to show its current status and sent to all manual holders.

4.2.5 A Master Copy of the manual is held by QA and uncontrolled copies, marked UNCONTROLLED, may be issued to visiting auditors and major clients under control of QA.

4.2.6 This manual is supported by a range of Quality Operating Procedures which are available to authorised Third Parties for inspection and assessment.

Quality Manual

Page 8 of 23 pages
Issue number of page: First   Date of issue: 1.2.93
Date of reissue: N/A   Authority for issue:
For reason for reissue see Amendment record, Section 3.3

4.3   Contract review

4.3.1 The control and review of our sales contracts are defined in our Contract Initiation and Review Procedure.

4.3.2 It is the duty of the Directors to maintain close contact with our customers.

4.3.3 Orders are taken into the company only after careful consideration of our ability to meet all requirements.

4.3.4 Major customers are asked to give advance notice of substantial increases in orders or of prospective change to our operating practices to enable us to assess our capability to deal with them.

4.3.5 All procurement, manufacture and supply is to specifications.

4.3.6 Customers are consulted on any foreseeable change to specifications.

4.3.7 Customers' orders are originated and processed with all due attention to detail and where necessary are queried with the customer for accuracy before progressing them.

4.3.8 Our contract procedures are reviewed at least annually.

Quality Manual

Page 9 of 23 pages
Issue number of page: First   Date of issue: 1.2.93
Date of reissue: N/A Authority for issue:
For reason for reissue see Amendment record, Section 3.3

4.4   Document control

4.4.1 Procedures shall be maintained to ensure that documents are originated, amended and reissued to a controlled and authorised system.

4.4.2 These procedures shall ensure that only correct, current editions of relevant documents are available where and when they are needed.

4.4.3 Records shall be maintained of all changes, updates and replacements to essential documents.

4.4.4 Change or pending change to customers' requirements, specifications and contractual requirements shall be via the Board with the approval of Quality Assurance.

Quality Manual

Page 10 of 23 pages
Issue number of page: First   Date of issue: 1.2.93
Date of reissue: N/A   Authority for issue:
For reason for reissue see Amendment record, Section 3.3

4.5   Purchasing

4.5.1   For all supplies of process raw materials, purchasing orders shall clearly state precise identification of the requirements.

4.5.2   Such orders shall refer to the precise materials ordered or to their current, approved specification code number or other clear identifier.

4.5.3   Every major supplier and subcontractor has been assessed and approved, with suitable controls to maintain the standards demanded. A list of approved suppliers and subcontractors has been drawn up and is maintained.

4.5.4   A system shall be used for continual assessment of each supplier and subcontractor on a regular basis.

4.5.5   Suppliers and subcontractors shall be reviewed in the Management Review.

4.5.6   Appropriate action shall be taken with suppliers and subcontractors found defaulting through review.

4.5.7   All process consumables shall be purchased to specification.

4.5.8   Consignments shall be verified for compliance with specification on arrival.

4.5.9   Nonconforming consigments shall be quarantined for further investigation before disposition.

4.5.10 Disposition shall be the responsibility of the Management Representative for BS 5750.

4.5.11 Where specified in contracts, the customer or his representative is given the right to verify at source or upon receipt that purchased product conforms to specified requirements. Verification by the customer does not absolve us of the responsibility to provide acceptable product nor does it preclude subsequent rejection. If the customer or his representative elects to carry out verification, this is not used by us as evidence of effective control of quality by the subcontractor.

Quality Manual

Page 11 of 23 pages
Issue number of page: First   Date of issue: 1.2.93
Date of reissue: N/A   Authority for issue:
For reason for reissue see Amendment record, Section 3.3

4.6   Purchaser supplied product

4.6.1 Certain customers supply materials for use in their products only, for example, packaging materials marked with their own print.

4.6.2 Such materials shall be treated as if we had purchased them and are subject to the same checks on receipt, the same preservation in storage and the same tests of function.

4.6.3 At any stage where customers' material shows non-conformity it shall be quarantined and the situation reported immediatedly to the customer.

4.6.4 Purchaser supplied material shall be pulled into our system of stock control.

4.6.5 Purchaser supplied material shall be stored in a manner that enables it to be readily identified.

Quality Manual

Page 12 of 23 pages
Issue number of page: First   Date of issue: 1.2.93
Date of reissue: N/A   Authority for issue:
For reason for reissue see Amendment record, Section 3.3

4.7   Product identification and traceability

4.7.1 All products purchased or 'purchaser supplied' shall carry identification from the supplier and be accompanied by documentation regarding source.

4.7.2 The packaging of all products manufactured by us shall be marked with a batch or date code which traces to day of manufacture.

4.7.3 The system shall afford traceability to date of manufacture for all products.

4.7.4 Where feasible, traceability to source shall also be afforded through our quality records.

4.7.5 On despatch of finished product to customers, the following records shall be maintained beyond the commercial shelf life of the products as additional aids to traceability:
   – daily production and quality records
   – stock records showing specific materials in use on specific dates.

Quality Manual

Page 13 of 23 pages
Issue number of page: First   Date of issue: 1.2.93
Date of reissue: N/A   Authority for issue:
For reason for reissue see Amendment record, Section 3.3

4.8   Process control

4.8.1 Work instructions (where necessary documented) shall be available to all personnel.

4.8.2 All work shall be carried out to procedures which are formally defined.

4.8.3 Equipment and materials for use shall be assessed for condition and compatibility with requirements.

4.8.4 The important variables during all processes shall be monitored and minimised.

4.8.5 Specifications shall be used to define acceptance criteria for all primary raw materials and for all product.

4.8.6 Special processes (if any) shall be subject to particularly stringent monitoring to provide evidence of control.

4.8.7 All areas used for processing or storage of materials shall be maintained in conditions that avoid contamination, loss of identity and damage.

4.8.8 Waste shall be disposed of in a timely and safe manner.

4.8.9 All product development, process development and production shall be carried out in conformance with the *Food Safety Act* 1990 and appropriate Regulations and to the requirements of Good Manufacturing Practice as defined by appropriate bodies such as IFST and the Leatherhead and Campden Food Research Associations.

Quality Manual

Page 14 of 23 pages
Issue number of page: First   Date of issue: 1.2.93
Date of reissue: N/A   Authority for issue:
For reason for reissue see Amendment record, Section 3.3

4.9   Inspection and testing

4.9.1   Receiving inspection and testing

4.9.1.1 Appropriate inspection shall be applied to incoming goods, depending on supplier rating.

4.9.1.2 Samples of incoming goods shall be drawn and checked according to specifications held by QA.

4.9.1.3 If approved, goods shall be accepted to store.

4.9.1.4 If rejected, the supplier shall be contacted to collect them. In the interim, rejected goods shall be quarantined.

4.9.1.5 Should verified goods subsequently be rejected, for example, during production, they shall be diverted from process and quarantined.

4.9.2   In-process inspection and testing

4.9.2.1 All employees shall be responsible for the quality of work they produce. In the production areas, a quality inspector shall monitor the processes.

4.9.2.2 Operators shall be trained and encouraged to report deviations from the norm to supervision.

4.9.2.3 Rework, scrap and problems shall be recorded and QA analysis carried out.

4.9.2.4 Appropriate process variables shall be identified and inspected and tested to written procedures.

4.9.3   Final inspection and testing

4.9.3.1 The satisfactory completion of all tests and records shall enable product to pass to final stage packaging, palletisation and despatch.

4.9.3.2 Approval for shipping of final product shall be conferred by QA.

4.9.3.3 If products require client witness of production and testing, the client's representative(s) shall be afforded every facility to that end.

4.9.4   Inspection and test records
4.9.4.1 Records shall be available for all inspection and test stages.
4.9.4.2 Only the personnel authorised to do so shall carry out and
        approve tests.

Quality Manual

Page 15 of 23 pages
Issue number of page: First   Date of issue: 1.2.93
Date of reissue: N/A   Authority for issue:
For reason for reissue see Amendment Record, Section 3.3

4.10   Inspection, measuring and test equipment

4.10.1 All measuring and test equipment with a critical bearing on quality shall be controlled and in a known state of calibration.

4.10.2 Calibration shall be carried out to a prescribed procedure in a suitable environment to nationally traceable standards.

4.10.3 All equipment shall be listed in a calibration log. This shall list the accuracy required, the frequency and the status of the equipment.

4.10.4 Test and measuring equipment with a subcritical bearing on quality shall be monitored and checked systematically.

4.10.5 Test and measuring equipment under formal calibration shall also be monitored and checked systematically for continuing fitness for purpose between calibrations.

4.10.6 It shall be the responsibility of everyone using equipment to see that it carries identification of calibration status.

4.10.7 It shall be the responsibility of the Management Representative for BS 5750 to ensure that the calibration of all listed equipment is maintained.

4.10.8 Planned maintenance of key processing equipment shall be operated to avoid unforseen breakdowns and to ensure its continued fitness for use.

4.10.9 If an instrument is found to have slipped out of calibration is shall be the responsibility of the Management Representative to examine the product quality implications of the nonconformance and to take appropriate remedial action.

Quality Manual

Page 16 of 23 pages
Issue number of page: First   Date of issue: 1.2.93
Date of reissue: N/A   Authority for issue:
For reason for reissue see Amendment record, Section 3.3

4.11   Inspection and test status

4.11.1 All documentation in use shall carry indication of its status.

4.11.2 All process materials and products shall carry either identification marks, labels or distinctive containers showing their status or be identifiable by their in-plant situation in semi-continuous production within enclosed plant.

4.11.3 All measuring and test equipment under formal calibration shall carry indication of its calibration status.

4.11.4 All nonconforming material and product shall be segregated and identified with QUARANTINE labels marked with a reference number or other means of tracing the material to a corrective action log maintained by QA.

Quality Manual

Page 17 of 23 pages
Issue number of page: First   Date of issue: 1.2.93
Date of reissue: N/A   Authority for issue:
For reason for reissue see Amendment record, Section 3.3

4.12   Control of nonconforming product

4.12.1 Goods received from suppliers and found to be non-conforming shall be quarantined in a suitable area and labelled as such and not called for use.

4.12.2 Goods in process and finished goods found to be non-conforming shall be quarantined and labelled as such and held for investigation.

4.12.3 All nonconformances shall be reported and trends analysed by QA and reviewed under the Management Review.

4.12.4 Disposition of quarantined goods shall only be decided by the Quality Manager or appointed delegate.

4.12.5 Records shall be maintained for all rework, regrade, concession and scrap.

Quality Manual

Page 18 of 23 pages
Issue number of page: First   Date of issue: 1.2.93
Date of reissue: N/A   Authority for issue:
For reason for reissue see Amendment record, Section 3.3

4.13   Corrective action

4.13.1 Corrective action shall arise from any situation found to conflict with quality.

4.13.2 All means at the disposal of management and staff shall be used to correct any such situation.

4.13.3 Details of nonconformances requiring corrective action shall be entered to a 'Corrective Action' form issued by Quality Assurance.

4.13.4 The Management Representative for BS 5750 and the relevant Departmental Manager shall sign off the document.

4.13.5 The same two managers shall then establish whether a permanent change in procedures is required to prevent a recurrence and issue an appropriate document amendment.

4.13.6 Customer complaints shall fall within the scope of action defined in these paragraphs.

4.13.7 Nonconformances requiring corrective action may be raised by any member of staff. They may result from audits, from reviews or from direct observation.

4.13.8 The effectiveness of all procedures for corrective action shall be monitored as part of the scheduled audit of the quality system and in management reviews.

Quality Manual

Page 19 of 23 pages
Issue number of page: First   Date of issue: 1.2.93
Date of reissue: N/A   Authority for issue:
For reason for reissue see Amendment record, Section 3.3

4.14   Handling, storage, packaging and delivery

4.14.1 Operating procedures or sub-manuals shall be issued to cover storage, handling, packaging and despatch and be supplemented by contractual requirements as necessary.

4.14.2 Instructions shall be reinforced with wall posters and hand-outs as necessary.

4.14.3 Attention of fork lift drivers, who shall be formally trained, shall be drawn to safe handling and storage procedures.

4.14.4 Storage facilities shall be maintained in correct condition for the products contained.

4.14.5 As far as commercially practicable, a 'First In, First Out' policy shall be maintained and process materials shall be ordered and finished products be manufactured 'Just In Time' to satisfy customers' orders.

4.14.6 Packaging, including all labelling and accompanying documentation, shall be under the surveillance of QA.

4.14.7 Final packaging for transportation shall be to company/customer specification or to recognised shipping procedures according to contract.

4.14.8 Product delivery shall be in clean, dry vehicles dedicated to handling foods and equipped with temperature control appropriate to the class of product conveyed.

Quality Manual

Page 20 of 23 pages
Issue number of page: First   Date of issue: 1.2.93
Date of reissue: N/A   Authority for issue:
For reason for reissue see Amendment record, Section 3.3

4.15   Quality records

4.15.1 Quality records shall be maintained to give evidence that the management system for the company is operating effectively.

4.15.2 Each manager and supervisor shall be responsible for ensuring that his/her department can establish that work has been carried out as required and that the company's and the customers' requirements have been complied with.

4.15.3 Quality records shall be retained for the necessary time to comply with legal and customer requirements and the retention period stated on each.

4.15.4 Records shall be retained in the department most suited to them or in a designated records room.

4.15.5 The storage environment for paper records shall be clean, dry, secure and warm to maintain them in good condition through their stated storage period.

4.15.6 Records held exclusively on computer readable material shall have back-up copies as a means of reconstruction in case of file damage or loss.

4.15.7 Quality records shall be clearly headed to indicate their purpose and their retention period.

Quality Manual

Page 21 of 23 pages
Issue number of page: First   Date of issue: 1.2.93
Date of reissue: N/A   Authority for issue:
For reason for reissue see Amendment record, Section 3.3

4.16   Internal quality audits

4.16.1 Compliance of the company's operating procedures and methods to BS 5750 shall be audited every month or more frequently as may be directed by the Board.

4.16.2 A forward audit programme shall be pre-announced to all relevant managers, areas or functions.

4.16.3 Trained auditors shall be used.

4.16.4 All audits shall be recorded.

4.16.5 The Quality Assurance function shall be audited by a team selected by the Managing Director or the Production Director.

4.16.6 The policy, as far as practicable, shall be that the auditor shall be independent of the area being audited but at all times shall be accompanied by a representative of the audited area as part of the audit team.

4.16.7 All nonconformances found during an audit shall be reported to the responsible manager and agreed at the time of audit.

4.16.8 Corrective actions resulting from the audit shall be reported to the Managing Director if the necessary action has not been taken within 15 days.

4.16.9 Audits and follow-up actions shall be reviewed at the following Management Review or more frequently if necessary.

Quality Manual

Page 22 of 23 pages
Issue number of page: First   Date of issue: 1.2.93
Date of reissue: N/A   Authority for issue:
For reason for reissue see Amendment record, Section 3.3

4.17   Training

4.17.1 Each Departmental Manager and Supervisor shall be responsible for ensuring that on a regular basis training carried out and training deemed necessary are recorded on a Training Assessment Log for each employee in his/her control.

4.17.2 Training Assessment Logs shall be issued and collected by an acting Training Officer who shall also make arrangements with the managers to carry out or have training carried out, internally or externally.

4.17.3 Each Manager shall be authorised to nominate an Instructor for the area(s) under his/her control if wished and thus ensure that there is a means of training everyone in the business to the levels necessary for their tasks.

4.17.4 The Training Officer, through his/her training programme, shall keep in touch with training courses and seminars and advise management of them as necessary. Equally, managers and staff shall be encouraged to suggest suitable training as they become aware of it.

Quality Manual

Page 23 of 23 pages
Issue number of page: First   Date of issue: 1.2.93
Date of reissue: N/A   Authority for issue:
For reason for reissue see Amendment record, Section 3.3

4.18   Statistical techniques

4.18.1 The company currently uses simple, basic statistical techniques to control its operations as appropriate, for example, product samples of four units are measured for variables such as net weights and container seal thickness at regular intervals. Sample averages, ranges and standard deviations are calculated and entered to control charts.

4.18.2 If justified by scale of production, the company shall obtain suitable advice, training and equipment to operate a more extensive SPC (Statistical Process Control) system.

Awareness seminar for BS 5750/ISO 9000

Guidelines for the use of this appendix

1 In this appendix an outline is given of a typical half day awareness seminar on BS 5750 which we deliver to companies in a range of industries.
2 It takes the form of a series of short statements for direct conversion to acetates for display using an overhead projector.
3 The material can be readily adapted to individual requirements though no major adaptation should be necessary.
4 The seminar is interactive as it involves the participants in five syndicate tasks devised to encourage them to apply the principles of BS 5750 to their own company.
5 Even at this very early stage of a company's interest in BS 5750, such involvement is highly beneficial.
6 The syndicate tasks should not be deferred to the end of proceedings but introduced as soon as the relevant topic has been discussed, in order to maintain interest and encourage interaction among the candidates and to prevent prolonged lecturing.
7 If the seminar has been successful, candidates should leave it with the knowledge that they have contributed positively to the proceedings and feeling, 'Yes, we can do it!'.

Acetate 1

BS 5750/ISO 9000
A half day awareness seminar

Contents

1 Introduction to BS 5750

2 Preparation for BS 5750

3 The practical application of BS 5750 to your company

4 The Documented Quality System

Acetate 2

BS 5750, Part 1, 2 or 3: which one to aim for?

BS 5750, Part 1 is 'for use when conformance to specified requirements is to be assured by the supplier during several stages which include design/ development, production, installation and servicing'.

BS 5750, Part 2 is 'for use when conformance to specified requirements is to be asssured by a company during production and installation'.

BS 5750, Part 3 is 'for use when conformance to specified requirements is to be assured by a company solely at final inspection and test'.

Part 2 covers most manufacturing and many service firms.

Therefore, unless a firm has a decided design input, or is inspecting finished product only, it should be aiming for BS 5750, Part 2.

Acetate 3

BS 5750: clauses of Parts 1 and 2

Part 1	Part 2	Clause heading
4.1	4.1	Management responsibility
4.2	4.2	Quality system
4.3	4.3	Contract review
4.4	N/A	Design control
4.5	4.4	Document control
4.6	4.5	Purchasing
4.7	4.6	Purchaser supplied product
4.8	4.7	Product identification and traceability
4.9	4.8	Process control
4.10	4.9	Inspection and testing
4.11	4.10	Inspection, measuring and test equipment
4.12	4.11	Inspection and test status
4.13	4.12	Control of nonconforming product
4.14	4.13	Corrective action
4.15	4.14	Handling, storage, packaging and delivery
4.16	4.15	Quality records
4.17	4.16	Internal quality audits
4.18	4.17	Training
4.19	N/A	Servicing
4.20	4.18	Statistical techniques

Acetate 4

First syndicate task

Over the next fifteen minutes tackle the two
questions below in your team. Appoint one of the
group to list your responses then please return for
discussion.

1 Suggest reasons why a firm might *not* want to go
for BS 5750.

2 What do you suppose are the biggest fears
companies have about going for BS 5750?

_____

3 How can these fears be overcome? **(Open
discussion)**

196

Acetate 5

Reasons for progressing to BS 5750

1 Better supplier performance through regular monitoring of their performance.
2 Own operations more efficient.
3 Improved relations with customers. Some demand BS 5750.
4 BS 5750 logo: a marketing plus.
5 Possible new markets through BS 5750.
6 Likelier to hold existing markets.
7 Mitigation of risk from customer complaints and claims.
8 European and general export marketing improved through EN 29000/BS 5750.
9 Helps to gain the Kitemark if desired.
10 BS 5750 can carry over to other areas of a business such as:
   – financial control
   – marketing
   – health & safety
   – the environment.

This takes one step towards Total Quality Management.

Acetate 6

Second syndicate task

Over the next fifteen minutes tackle the following
tasks in your team. Appoint one of your group to list
your responses then please return for discussion.

Examine and discuss the list of proposed reasons for
progressing to BS 5750.

1 Delete or amend any that you consider unfair or
   overpitched. Summarise your findings.

2 See if you can identify at least one new reason that
   might apply within your group.

Acetate 7

BS 5750/ISO 9000/EN 29000

For all practical purposes BS 5750, ISO 9000 and EN 29000 are the same thing.

EN 29000 may mean more to a European than BS 5750.

ISO 9000 may mean more to someone in the USA or Japan (for example) than BS 5750.

Both ISO 9000 and EN 29000 are automatically given to a company when registered to BS 5750.

There is no extra charge for ISO 9000 and EN 29000.

ISO 9000 and EN 29000 can improve export marketing.

Acetate 8

Third syndicate task

Over the next fifteen minutes tackle the following
tasks in your team. Appoint a one of your group to
list your responses then please return for discussion.

Examine and discuss the short paper on
BS 5750/EN 29000 and then:

without giving any trade secrets away, try to give
and explain one *concrete* example of how your factory
or group could benefit from BS 5750 accreditation.

This could be an example from within the areas listed
below but do not feel restricted to these examples
only:

increased plant utilisation

new product(s)

increased market, home or overseas

defence of existing market from 'Europredators'

improved in-house efficiency.

Acetate 9

BS 5750: costs – initial and on-going

1 Consultancy fees if using consultants. May be grant aided.

2 Assessment fee. Charged by the body which assesses you for registration to BS 5750.

3 Annual registration/surveillance fee. Charged by the assessing company which inspects you about twice a year to maintain registration.

4 The cost of management and staff time to install and operate BS 5750.

5 Possible additional costs, for example:
   – word processor
   – special training (may be grant aided)
   – special services, for example, visiting calibration engineer.

Acetate 10

Talking point No. 1

BS 5750: how to prepare *everyone* in the company for it

Discussion points for seminar

1 Motivation

Of the following, whom do you consider are generally found to be the hardest to motivate to a sustained drive to and beyond BS 5750 accreditation:

– **top management** (for example, Board)

– **senior management** (for example, Fgm, Production Manager, QA Manager, Chief Eng'r)

– **line supervisors**

– **line operators?**

2 What can we learn from this?

Open discussion

3 Preparing everyone in your company for BS 5750. Some pointers:
participation by all, pre-assessment *and after*

training

quality control *v* quality assurance.

Acetate 11

Fourth syndicate task

Over the next fifteen minutes tackle the following tasks in your team. Appoint a member of the group to list your responses then please return for discussion.

Examine and discuss the paper **BS 5750: how to prepare everyone for it**.

Then, with reference to BS 5750, put forward proposals on how to motivate, prepare, train and involve people from the following groups within your company:

– **top management** (for example, Board)

– **senior management** (for example, Production Manager, QA Manager, Purchasing Manager)

– **supervisors**

– **line operators.**

Acetate 12

BS 5750 as an aid to Total Quality Management (TQM)

Plan 1 Some firms develop TQM or a comparable system *first*, then progress to BS 5750.

Plan 2 Others *reverse* the above order, going for BS 5750 first and then considering whether further development is necessary.

Both systems have their merits.

Plan 2: BS 5750 first

Perceived/claimed disadvantages of BS 5750
1 Currently oriented to manufacturing and product control only.
2 No great 'philosophical/cultural change' undergone by company.
3 Too rigid.

Perceived/claimed advantages of BS 5750
1 Highly definitive. Customers know exactly where they stand.
2 Evolves naturally from GMP and similar systems which are normally operative in well controlled firms.
3 Principles of BS 5750 *can* be extended beyond manufacturing, for example, to distribution. Why not also to marketing, financial control and so on?
4 If paragraph 3 is developed enthusiastically, Total Quality Commitment begins to develop.

Acetate 13

Fifth syndicate task

Over the next twenty minutes tackle the following tasks in your team. Appoint a member of your group to list your responses then please return for discussion.

Examine and discuss the paper **BS 5750 as an aid to TQM** and then answer the questions below.

1 Name three ways in which BS 5750 principles might usefully be applied in your company in a drive to TQM.

2 Assuming that manuals defining marketing, financial control and general administration have been drawn up in a TQM programme, suggest the skeleton of a procedure for any *one* of the following:

   a) (marketing) – a regional test launch of a new product

   b) (financial control) – budgetary control of that new product

   c) (administration) – answering the telephone efficiently and courteously at all times. (Do not underestimate this one. Many orders are lost at this stage.)

Internal quality audit checklists for clauses of BS 5750, Part 2/ISO 9002

Guidelines to use of this appendix

1 The checklists address a company's 'self auditing' requirements against each of the 18 clauses of BS 5750, Part 2.
2 They encourage auditing by function, for example, by contract control, purchasing control, process control and so on, as well as by department of the company. This is particularly useful in small to medium size companies who may not have many departments.
3 The checklists are 'ready for use' by quality auditors who are operating the BS 5750 system of internal quality auditing.
4 Each begins by asking whether there is a written procedure defining the function. Remember that this does not always demand the answer 'Yes'. If the function is relatively minor in your business and already adequately addressed in your Master Quality Manual, answer accordingly and move on to the next question.
5 Do not feel bound to follow these checklists to the letter. It is recommended that you adapt them to your own precise needs with experience.
6 However, if you have a problem with your quality system in its emergent phase, these checklists will reveal it. Therefore do not amend them till you have given them a good try.
7 You may also want to consider expanding them in certain key areas such as process control. See Appendix 4 for guidance on this.

4.1   Management review

1 Is there a written procedure defining this clause of BS 5750? **Yes/No**.
2 If **No**, is there a need for one? **Comment**.
3 If **Yes**, is it clear and operable by the company? **Comment**.
4 Is there a written quality policy statement? **Verify**.
5 Is it realistic? **Read and comment**.
6 Has it been made available for everyone in the company to read? **Verify**.
7 Is there a written 'Management Structure'? **Check**.
8 Is it accurate and up to date? **Discusswith appropriate people and comment**.
9 Is there a nominated Management Representative for BS 5750? **Check**.
10 And a deputy? **Check**.
11 Are the 'verification resources and personnel' listed? **Check**.
12 Are they appropriate? **Examine and comment**.
13 Are Management Reviews of the quality system being held? **Check**.
14 At an appropriate frequency? **Check**.
15 Are they minuted? **Check**.
16 Do appropriate clauses of BS 5750 and other key quality matters come under regular review? **Check**.
17 Does the Chairman or equivalent chair the reviews? **Check**.

4.2   Quality System

1 Is there a written procedure defining this clause of BS 5750? **Yes/No**.
2 If **No**, is there a need for one? **Comment**.
3 If **Yes**, is it clear and operable by the company? **Comment**.
4 Does it adequately address the requirements of BS 5750: 1987, Part 2/ISO 9002? **Check** the Quality Manual and any two procedures.
5 Is the list of procedures sufficient to define the system fully? **Examine** and comment.
6 Are the available quality records sufficient to define the system fully? **Examine** and comment.
7 Is the system active? **Examine** any two quality records.
8 Is it clear who is responsible for what? **Examine** section 1 of the manual and comment.
9 Are effective quality audits being carried out? **Examine** the file and comment.

4.3 Control of contracts

1 **Is there a written procedure defining this clause of BS 5750? Yes/No**.
2 If **No**, is there a need for one? **Comment**.
3 If **Yes**, is it clear and operable by the company? **Comment**.
4 Are new orders (contracts) carefully cross checked? **Check** two recent or current contracts.
5 Are the customer's QA requirements determined? **Check** two instances.
6 Are all important contract documents cross checked by an appropriate person before release? **Check** two contracts.
7 Are records of orders, modifications and problems held in satisfactory condition? **Check** the filing system.
8 Where customers' material is processed are there clearly defined arrangements for dealing with problems and queries? **Check** any recent contract where this situation is known to have arisen.
9 Is there a system for negotiating concessions with customers? **Check**.
10 Are concessions being correctly negotiated with customers? **Check** concession file.
11 Are materials and services provided under contracts clearly identified (for example by specification reference number or alternative method)? **Check** any two recent contracts.
12 Is contract control reviewed under the management review? **Check** the minutes of the management review.

4.4   Document control

1   Is there a written procedure defining this clause of BS 5750? **Yes/No**.
2   If **No**, is there a need for one? **Comment**.
3   If **Yes**, is it clear and operable by the company? **Comment**.
4   Does it list all quality documents controlling the company? **Verify**.
5   Are there clear arrangements for controlling and updating controlled documents? **Check**.
6   And externally controlled documents? **Check**.
7   Are quality documents clearly headed? **Check** one procedure and one quality record.
8   Are they of valid current issue? **Check** another two procedures and two quality records.
9   Is Document Control under review? **Verify**.
10 Is it clear who controls documents? **Verify**.

4.5   Purchasing

1 Is there a written procedure defining this clause of BS 5750? **Yes/No**.
2 If **No**, is there a need for one? **Comment**.
3 If **Yes**, is it clear and operable by the company? **Comment**.
4 Do purchase orders state precise identification of requirements? **Check** two orders for:
   – clear definition of materials ordered
   – price
   – delivery instructions
   – any special instructions for example, delivery time and so on.
5 Is raising of purchase orders limited to defined people/functions? **Check**.
6 Is there a 'two tier' purchasing system whereby orders up to a stated value may be processed by relatively junior staff whereas larger ones are restricted to senior management? **Check**.
7 Are **all** orders of process consumables recorded in writing? **Check** four.
8 Do the purchasing people consider the system workable? **Interview** them.
9 Are the purchasing people adequately resourced? **Ascertain**.
10 Is all purchased stock quality inspected on arrival? **Check** two orders.
11 Is this clearly documented and recorded? **Check** two orders.
12 Is nonconforming purchased stock quarantined? **Check** quarantine area and records.
13 Is there a list of approved suppliers/subcontractors? **Examine** and comment.
14 If so is it up to date and accurate? **Examine** and comment.
15 Is there a system for quality grading suppliers/subcontractors? **Examine** and comment.
16 If so, is it practical and workable? **Examine** and comment.
17 Is it in regular operation? **Examine** two records.
18 Is quality inspection of purchased goods related to the quality status of suppliers? **Examine**.
19 Have all major suppliers/subcontractors been sent a quality questionnaire? **Check** and comment.
20 If so have all returned them? **Check**.
21 Do purchasing documents and procedures refer to and make use of material specifications? **Ascertain**.
22 If **Yes** to 21, are the specifications useful to purchasing staff by being well written and clear? **Check**.
23 If **Yes** to 22, are the specifications up to date and valid? **Check**.

24 If **No** to 21 are there valid alternatives to specifications? **Ascertain and list them as available**, for example, 'Purchased against an approved sample'. 'Purchased on the basis of a Certificate of Conformity from the supplier'.

25 Are there specifications or equivalent for all process consumables? **Check**.

4.6   Purchaser supplied product

1 **Does this situation arise in the company? Comment**.
2 If so, is there a written procedure defining this clause of BS 5750? **Yes/No**.
3 If **No**, is there a need for one? **Comment**.
4 If **Yes**, is it clear and operable by the company? **Comment**.
5 Does the verification, storage, handling and so on of this product differ from that of this company's own product? **Examine** and comment.
6 If not, are the existing company methods adequate to deal with it? **Examine** and comment.
7 Does the customer request any special controls for this material, for example, does he or she ask for stock control returns, quality reports and so on? **Check** and comment.
8 If so, are arrangements for supplying such information to his or her satisfaction? **Examine** and comment.

4.7   Product identification and traceability

1 **Is there a written procedure defining this clause of BS 5750? Yes/No.**
2 If **No**, is there a need for one? **Comment**.
3 If **Yes**, is it clear and operable by the company? **Comment**.
4 Does it address all the company's products and services? **Verify**.
5 Are the company's packaged products clearly marked or labelled to show their identity? **Check** any two.
6 Are the packages marked with a batch number or equivalent traceability mark, for example, an expiry date? **Check** any two.
7 Do they afford traceability to (at least) date of manufacture? **Comment**.
8 Are labels, batch numbers and so on clearly legible? **Examine** any two.
9 Do they define the products clearly? **Comment**.
10 Are labels and batch codes adequately protected from defacement during transit? **Examine**.
11 Are there appropriate 'traceability' arrangements for products or sevices other than packaged product supplied by the company, for example. bulk deliveries, on-site treatments, reports, software? **Check** and comment.
12 Have suppliers been asked to mark a batch number or equivalent traceability mark to product supplied to the company? **Check** two quality questionnaires.
13 Have they complied with the request? **Check** two responses.
14 If required to recall product, would the traceability records enable this to be done effectively? **Conduct** a dummy 'recall'.
15 Is there a written 'recall' procedure? **Yes/No**.
16 If **No** to 15, is there a need for one? **Yes/No**.

4.8   Process control

Comment: the questions listed below refer to processes. Companies in the service sector should substitute 'service' for 'process' wherever it appears and use all the questions except 8 and 9 to audit their service provision.

1 Is there a written procedure defining this clause of BS 5750? **Yes/No**.
2 If **No**, is there a need for one? **Comment**.
3 If **Yes**, is it clear and operable by the company? **Comment**.
4 Are there appropriate documented work instructions for all processes? **Check** two.
5 Are they available where they are needed? **Comment**.
6 Do they define standards of workmanship and service in writing where relevant? **Check** one operating procedure in depth.
7 Are processes effectively monitored and controlled? **Check** one in depth.
8 Are there any 'special processes' as defined by BS 5750? **Comment**.
9 If so, are there appropriate recorded controls on them? **Check** one in depth.
10 Is there a system for reviewing and updating control documents? **Check**.
11 Are process control records consistently and regularly completed? **Check** two current records.

4.9   Inspection and testing

1 Is there a written procedure defining this clause of BS 5750? **Yes/No**.
2 If **No**, is there a need for one? **Comment**.
3 If **Yes**, is it clear and operable by the company? **Comment**.
4 If relevant does it cover tests and so on carried out on materials before delivery to the company? **Check**.
5 Does it cover verifications and tests carried out on incoming deliveries? **Check**.
6 Are these verifications and tests adequate as verifiers of incoming product quality? **Examine** and comment.
7 If **No** to 6, what additional controls are necessary? **List** them.
8 Is the extent of verification and testing of incoming material related to the quality status of suppliers? **Examine** and comment.
9 If **No** to 8, would there be any advantage from introducing such a system? **Yes/No**.
10 Does the procedure cover testing of processes? **Check**.
11 Does it cover finished goods or services? **Check**.
12 Are there suitable arrangements for holding materials pending clearance through tests and so on? **Check**.
13 Does the company operate 'positive release' of finished product or service? **Check** and comment.
14 If not, is there a requirement or advantage from doing so? **Consider and comment.**
15 Are test and inspection records appropriate and clear? **Check** two.
16 Are they being consistently completed? **Check** two current records.
17 Are completed records being held for an appropriate time? **Check** two.

4.10   Calibration of test and measuring equipment

1 Is there a written procedure defining this clause of BS 5750? **Yes/No**.
2 If **No**, is there a need for one? **Comment**.
3 If **Yes**, is it clear and operable by the company? **Comment**.
4 Does it differentiate clearly between equipment under formal calibration and equipment not under formal calibration? **Check**.
5 If so, has the company's equipment been accurately classified into the appropriate categories? **Check**.
6 Is the classification acceptable to all relevant managers, for example, those engaged in process control? **Discuss**.
7 Is there a list of all equipment under formal calibration? **Check**.
8 Is there a list of all equipment not under formal calibration? **Check**.
9 Are both lists up to date? **Examine**.
10 Does the system allow for monitoring of formally calibrated equipment between calibrations? **Examine**.
11 Is all calibrated equipment in a state of formal calibration? **Examine** records.
12 Is all 'sub-critical' equipment undergoing regular monitoring? **Check** records.
13 Are all calibration and monitoring methods appropriate to the company's needs? **Discuss**.
14 Are instruments and so on labelled or otherwise identifiable as to their calibration or monitoring status? **Check** three.
15 Are appropriate master instruments held or accessible through a calibration subcontractor? **Check**.
16 Are instruments appropriately packaged and stored? **Check** two.
17 Are appropriate calibration and monitoring records maintained? **Check** them.
18 Is there a list of calibration subcontractors? **Check**.
19 If **No** to 18, is there a need for one? **Yes/No**.

4.11   Inspection and test status

1 Is there a written procedure defining this clause of BS 5750? **Yes/No**.
2 If **No**, is there a need for one? **Comment**.
3 If **Yes**, is it clear and operable by the company? **Comment**.
4 Is there a written procedure for identifying and dealing with product under quarantine? **Examine** and comment.
5 If so, is it clear and practical? **Read** and comment.
6 Is it being applied? **Examine** 'quarantined goods' register.
7 Is quarantined product clearly marked? **Examine** whether any is available and, if so, comment.
8 Is it readily traceable to a register, for example, by means of a unique identifying number marked to both the goods and the register? **Check** and comment.
9 Is there a dedicated quarantine area? **Comment**.
10 If so, is it appropriate? **Comment**.
11 If not, is there the space to institute one? **Examine** and comment.
12 If not, are arrangements for marking and segregating such material adequate? **Examine** and comment.
13 Is conforming material marked in any way to distinguish it from product awaiting test or otherwise 'frozen'? **Examine** and comment.
14 If not, is there a need to do so? **Examine** and comment.
15 On a tour of the premises is the distinction between conforming and 'frozen' product always totally clear? **Tour premises and comment**.

4.12   Control of nonconforming product or service

1 Is there a written procedure defining this clause of BS 5750? **Yes/No**.
2 If **No**, is there a need for one? **Comment**.
3 If **Yes**, is it clear and operable by the company? **Comment**.
4 Are there effective arrangements for segregating non-conforming product? **Check** on site.
5 Are there effective arrangements for identifying it (for example, by quarantine labels)? **Check** on site.
6 And tracing it to a log or record giving details? **Check**.
7 Is such material under responsible control? **Check** and state who controls it.
8 Who is responsible for disposition of nonconforming product? **Check** and state.
9 Are clear records kept of dispositions? **Check** two.
10 Do they distinguish between product accepted for release, product put to rework, product scrapped and product regraded to other outlets? **Check** another two.
11 Do records show these quantities? **Check** two.
12 Are these records in regular use? **Check** two recent incidents.
13 Is there written provision for seeking a customer concession as necessary? **Check**.
14 Is nonconformity under Management Review? **Check**.
15 Is appropriate consideration given to preventing a recurrence during nonconformance analysis? **Check** two incidents.

4.13   Corrective Action

1 Is there a written procedure defining this clause of BS 5750? **Yes/No**.
2 If **No**, is there a need for one? **Comment**.
3 If **Yes**, is it clear and operable by the company? **Comment**.
4 Is it up to date? **Read** it.
5 Is it being operated correctly? **Check** any two corrective action reports.
6 Is there evidence of consistent operation? **Check** the two most recent corrective action reports.
7 Is appropriate action taken on corrective actions? **Check** two incidents.
8 Are Corrective Action Request and Report forms available to all concerned? **Check**.
9 Are these forms being directed to the correct person to deal with them, for example, the Quality Representative? **Check**.
10 Is it clear that the forms should be directed to the Quality Representative or equivalent? **Read** it and amend it if necessary.
11 Are all corrective actions being correctly processed? **Check** two.
12 Are they all effectively closed off? **Check** two.

4.14.   Handling, storage, packaging and delivery

1 Is there a written procedure defining this clause of BS 5750? **Yes/No**.
2 If **No**, is there a need for one? **Comment**.
3 If **Yes**, is it clear and operable by the company? **Comment**.
4 Are handling methods appropriate and designed to prevent product damage? **Examine** in depth and comment.
5 Are materials and products correctly stored to avoid stress and other damage? **Check** on site.
6 If relevant, are there suitable environmental controls and records (for example, for temperature or humidity)? **Check** on site.
7 Are materials and product suitably identified and segregated in store? **Verify** on site.
8 Are there suitable arrangements for issuing materials on a First In, First Out (FIFO) basis where appropriate? **Check**.
9 Is the company holding appropriate stock levels? **Verify** on site or against records.
10 Is enough space allocated to handling and storage? **Yes/No**.
11 Are filling and packaging methods appropriate? **Verify** on site.
12 Does the company carry out its own product distribution? **Check**.
13 If so, are drivers appropriately certificated? **Check** two records.
14 Is vehicle maintenance well controlled and recorded? **Check**.
15 If distribution is partly or entirely subcontracted do the subcontractors possess appropriate credentials? **Verify**.
16 Does the company have contractual or other obligations for quality of product in transit to the consignee? **Examine** and state position.
17 If so, are these obligations being met? **Check** a current despatch.
18 Has formal training been provided for staff where necessary? **Examine** two training records, for example, for fork lift truck drivers.
19 If several consignments are to be carried on one vehicle are there suitable arrangements for segregating them and marking them clearly as to product, quantity, consignee and so on? **Check** such a load as available.
20 If **Yes** to 19, have steps been taken to maintain quality of goods, segregation, marking and so on all through transit? **Examine** as for 19.

4.15   Quality records

1 Is there a written procedure defining this clause of BS 5750? **Yes/No**.
2 If **No**, is there a need for one? **Comment**.
3 If **Yes**, is it clear and operable by the company? **Comment**.
4 Is there a list of current quality records? **Check**.
5 If so, is it up to date and accurate? **Examine** and comment.
6 Are quality records clearly marked as to purpose? **Examine** any two.
7 Is their retention period stated? **Examine** and comment.
8 Do the quality records serve their purpose effectively? **Examine** two and comment.

4.16   Internal quality auditing

1 Is there a written procedure defining this clause of BS 5750? **Yes/No**.
2 If **No**, is there a need for one? **Comment**.
3 If **Yes**, is it clear and operable by the company? **Comment**.
4 Have auditors been trained? **Discuss** and comment.
5 Is so, how and where? **Examine** and comment.
6 Is the auditing system in operation? **Examine** and comment.
7 Is there a formal programme of audits to be carried out? **Check**.
8 Are nonconformances found during audits being recorded? **Check**
9 And acted upon? **Check**.
10 Are realistic task completion dates being set? **Check**.
11 Are 'auditees' being given the opportunity to comment on audit findings? **Examine** any two audit or nonconformance reports and comment.
12 Are auditees always in agreement with audit findings? **Examine** two records.
13 Have any external audits to BS 5750 been carried out on the company? **Comment**.
14 If so, have they been recorded? **Examine** audit file and comment.
15 And acted upon? **Comment**.
16 Have any external audits to alternative systems been carried out on the company? **Comment**.
17 If so, have they been recorded? **Comment**.
18 And acted upon? **Comment**.

4.17   Training

1 Is there a written procedure defining this clause of BS 5750? **Yes/No**.
2 If **No**, is there a need for one? **Comment**.
3 If **Yes**, is it clear and operable by the company? **Comment**.
4 Is there a specialist Training Officer in the company? **Comment**.
5 If not, are there adequate arrangements for issuing and maintaining training records? **Examine** and comment.
6 Are the quality training requirements of people at all levels suitably identified? **Examine**.
7 Is there a training record for each person in the company with a quality involvement? **Examine**.
8 If so, does it provide for recording of people's previous education, experience and competence? **Examine**.
9 Does it provide for identification and recording of additional skills as they are acquired? **Examine**.
10 Are all training records complete and up to date? **Examine** at least two.
11 Have key people received formal training in BS 5750? **Examine**.
12 If not, have they received appropriate alternative training in BS 5750 e.g. by working along with consultants engaged by the company? **Examine** and comment.
13 Have all process and other hourly paid workers been made aware of BS 5750 and their contribution to its effective implementation? **Check**.
14 If so, how has this been done? **Check**.
15 Is it recorded on their records? **Check** any two records.

4.18   Statistics

1 Does the company operate formal statistical control of any of its operations? **Discuss and comment.**
2 If so, are the methods formally written up e.g. as a procedure or operating instruction? **Examine** and comment.
3 If so, are the methods used appropriate? **Examine** and comment based on own judgment or that of a specialist in such methods.
4 If no statistical control is operated, is there a case for doing so? **Examine** , discuss with appropriate staff and comment.
5 If no statistical control is operated, are existing methods of sampling etc affording suitable control? **Examine** and comment.
6 Is any external statistical work such as market research sub-contracted to specialist companies? **Yes/No.**
7 If so are these companies listed as approved subcontractors? **Yes/No**.

Internal quality audit checklists for process control

Guidelines to use of this appendix

1 First, put into operation the checklists of Appendix 3 which, by covering all 18 clauses of BS 5750, are intended to highlight deficiencies in a quality system during its development to compliance with the standard.
2 Some companies are content to continue with the functional audits of Appendix 3, adapting them to their own requirements with experience.
3 However as they are 'broadbrush' in approach, there is a case for developing additional, highly specific checklists to examine in detail aspects of important functions in the organisation.
4 One such function is process control. Suggestions are offered in this appendix for compiling checklists for specific aspects of process control in the food, fine chemical and healthcare industries which have demanding process control requirements.
5 The intention is to indicate lines of approach which can be adapted not only to other clauses of BS 5750 within those industries but also to industries other than those examined in this appendix.

Laboratory control

As a laboratory is frequently a critical element of process control in manufacturing and service industry companies, it is worthy of special attention through a specific audit checklist as set out below or on similar lines.

1 Are laboratory resources appropriate and well maintained? **Check** two instruments and two records.
2 Are quality records well maintained and clearly marked? **Check** two records controlling different aspects, for example, raw material analysis; process control analysis; and finished product analysis.
3 Is there a Laboratory Manual? **Comment**.
4 Is it clear and legible? **Read** and comment.
5 Does it cover all the company's methods of analysis? **Comment**.
6 Does it explain how 'primary standards' are controlled? **Comment.**
7 Are sampling methods appropriate? **Check**.
8 Are sampling and testing at all stages being carried out as stated in the Laboratory Manual or equivalent? **Check** one example from each stage.
9 Are the laboratory staff suitably qualified? **Verify**.
10 Are they suitably trained? **Verify**.
11 Is instrumental analysis carried out? **Comment**.
12 If so, has such equipment been competently commissioned to the company' requirements? **study** and comment.
13 Is laboratory equipment under appropriate calibration and monitoring? **examine** and comment.
14 If so, is it described under the company Calibration Procedure or in a separate procedure for laboratory equipment? **Comment**.
15 Is the laboratory subject to external quality auditing? **Comment**.
16 If so, is it to a formal third party scheme such as NAMAS? **Comment**.
17 Is 'good housekeeping' in evidence in the laboratory? **Comment**.
18 Is glassware and so on clean? **Comment**.
19 Are chemicals clearly labelled to purpose? **Comment**.
20 Are hazardous chemicals under appropriate control? **Examine** and **Comment**.
21 Is any analysis subcontracted? **Yes/No**.
22 If **Yes**, to 21, is the subcontractor of approved status? **Examine** and comment.
23 Is the subcontractor listed as an approved subcontractor to the company? **Yes/No**.

Control of good manufacturing practice and Due Diligence compliance

This is a critical aspect of the fine chemicals and related industries. The checklist below is for the food industry and can be adapted to industries of equivalent market sensitivity.

1 As well as the requirements of BS 5750, have the recommendations of the latest editions of the following documents been embodied in the QA system? **Yes/No**.

1.1 *Good Manufacturing Practice – A Guide to its Responsible Management*, Institute of Food Science and Technology,

1.2 *Quality System for the Food and Drink Industries*, Leatherhead Food Research Association.

2 Are all ingredients sourced from established suppliers who operate quality assurance? **Yes/No**.

3 Is careful consideration given to composition when developing new products, ensuring that legally prescribed compositional limits are met? **Comment**, describing arrangements.

4 Are product protection schedules in operation? **Describe**.

5 Do product labels conform with the Labelling of Food Regulations as amended and are they regularly monitored? **Yes/No**.

6 Are product net weights are controlled to the requirements of the *Weights and Measures Act*? **Yes/No**.

6.1 Minimum or averages system? **Comment**.

7 Is conformity of packaging materials with the *Materials in Contact with Food Regulations* verified? **Yes/No**.

8 Are raw materials, work in progress and finished product regularly tested and tasted? **Comment**.

9 Do product container codes afford traceability to date of production? **Yes/No**.

10 How does the company keep itself informed on developments in food law? **Comment**.

11 Are housekeeping, waste disposal, hygiene and plant cleaning systems in operation? **Yes/No**.

12 Are specifications defining materials, recipes and operating methods in use? **Yes/No**.

13 Are quality records maintained beyond the shelf life of products? **Yes/No**.

14 Is each day's production 'positively released' after scrutiny, by the Quality Manager or delegate, of relevant records? **Yes/No**.

15 Are packaging bar codes regularly verified for accuracy? **Yes/No**.

16 Is hygiene training to the requirements of the Food Act 1990 in operation? **Yes/No**.

Hygiene, housekeeping and pest control

This is a critical aspect of sensitive operations and extends well beyond the food and fine chemicals industries. The underlisted questions are addressed to the food industry but are readily adaptable to other situations demanding high aesthetic standards.

1 Are personal hygiene training records up to date? **Check** any two.
2 Is satisfactory personal hygiene in evidence? **Check** two operatives.
3 Is protective clothing being worn as appropriate? **Check** two operatives.
4 Are toilet and handwashing facilities appropriate? **Inspect** and comment.
5 In processing areas are there separate washing facilities for personnel and equipment? **Inspect** and comment.
6 Are formal product protection systems in operation (e.g metal detectors, covers, 'insectocutors', line sieves, line magnets) **Examine** and comment.
7 Are palletised goods 0.5 m away from walls? **Visit** store and comment.
8 Are well maintained bait trays in evidence? **Inspect** and comment.
9 Are they accessible? **Yes/No**.
10 Is there a pest 'sightings' log? ASK to see it.
11 If so, is it up to date? **Comment**.
12 Is pest control subcontracted? **Comment**.
13 If so, is the subcontractor efficient? **Discuss** and comment.
14 Are recommendations of the pest control subcontractor adopted by the company? **Examine** pest control file.
14 If so, is it described under the company Calibration Procedure or in a separate procedure for laboratory equipment? **Comment**.
15 Is the laboratory subject to external quality auditing? **Comment**.
16 If so, is it to a formal third party scheme such as NAMAS? **Comment**.
17 Is 'good housekeeping' in evidence in the laboratory? **Comment**.
18 Is glassware and so on clean? **Comment**.
19 Are chemicals clearly labelled to purpose? **Comment**.
20 Are hazardous chemicals under appropriate control? **Examine** and comment.
21 Is any analysis subcontracted? **Yes/No**.
22 If **Yes**, to 21 is the subcontractor of approved status? **Examine**

and comment.

23 Is the subcontractor listed as an approved subcontractor to the company? **Yes/No.**

Specimen multiple choice tests for use in awareness training for BS 5750/ISO 9000

Guidelines for the use of this appendix

1 Fifteen specimen multiple choice questions from our own house training manual are provided in this appendix as introduction to BS 5750 awareness.
2 They are based on the principles outlined on pages 53–5 of the main text which are probably worth rereading before tackling the questions.
3 Our perceptions of the correct responses are given on the final pages and we hope that you will not be in serious dispute with them once you have attempted the questions.
4 If you disagree with some of our responses this is not a problem as the resulting discussions during training sessions can be just as enlightening as the test itself.

Training for internal quality auditing to BS 5750
A multiple choice self test pack

Purpose

This is phase 2.2 of the assessment component of our training course on internal quality auditing to BS 5750. It consists of two parts.

1 Introduction (on this page). Read it carefully before attempting the questions.
2 A series of multiple choice questions on practical aspects of BS 5750.

Introduction

1 This self test pack is intended to help us assess your under-standing of auditing to BS 5750 following our short course. It is only one aspect of your overall assessment, counting for 15% of your final mark.
2 It consists of fifteen questions based on faults in the BS 5750 system of the practices of a notional food processing company 'Foodpro' in the following areas:
document control
control of identification and labelling of product
control of substandard product
control of test and measuring equipment
control of processes
control of purchasing
control of audits and reviews.
3 In each question there are three statements. Only one accurately describes a nonconformance against BS 5750 which you are asked to identify from the information provided. Read each question carefully and then, using the grid on the answer paper provided, list against each question number the response which you consider most accurately describes the nonconformance.
4 After your paper has been marked there will be an oral test worth ten marks based on the fifteen questions. You may have valid reasons for preferring alternative responses to some we have listed as correct and the resulting discussion can be more informative than the written test.

Appendix 5

Training for internal quality auditing to BS 5750

Multiple choice component   Time allowed: thirty minutes

Candidate: _____

Company: _____

Position: _____

Date: _____

Please give your responses here:

Question	Response	Question	Response	Question	Response
1	_____	6	_____	11	_____
2	_____	7	_____	12	_____
3	_____	8	_____	13	_____
4	_____	9	_____	14	_____
5	_____	10	_____	15	_____

For Examiner only:

Multiple choice mark: ☐

Oral mark: ☐

Total for component 2.2: ☐

Signed for MPA: _____

Date: _____

Question 1

The excerpt below from a Foodpro purchasing document could fail
BS 5750 because:

a) it does not provide enough information on the material ordered

b) it is not marked with the date of ordering

c) it is not signed by the Management Representative for BS 5750.

Supplier: G Smith and Sons Ltd, 27 High Street, Anytown,
Middlesex MH1 2RJ.

Order date: 21.4.93

Order No: 12556/93 (Please quote on all communications)

Please supply the following, carriage paid home:

Delivery date: on or before 5.5.93

Description	Spec No.	Unit price	Quantity	Total price
Sugar		£500.00 per tonne	4 tonnes	£2,000.00

Question 2

The excerpt overleaf from a Foodpro purchasing document could fail
BS 5750 because:

a) the goods are not clearly described

b) the goods are not adequately identified

c) the supplier is not clearly identified.

Supplier: Usual one   *Question 2 continued*

Order date: 21.4.93

Order No: 12556/93 (Please quote on all communications)

Please supply the following, carriage paid home:

Delivery date: on or before 5.5.93

Description	Spec No.	Unit price	Quantity	Total price
Liquid glucose	FP 104	£50.00 per	6 drums 205 l drum	£300.00

Question 3

The document below fails to conform to BS 5750 because:

a) it is not clear who was responsible for preparing and issuing it

b) the title is unclear

c) the number of pages in the document is not clearly stated.

Foodpro Ltd Page: 1 of 6

Title: Product sterilisation procedure Ref: SOP 8.1

Originated by: **Approved by**: JMC **Issue**: 2   **Date**: 21.01.93

Contents:

1 Description of steriliser p 1

2 Operation of steriliser p 3

Circulation:

Quality Representative

Manager, Sterilisation

Question 4

The undernoted completed Goods Received Note fails to conform to BS 5750 because:

a) the material has been accepted on insufficient evidence of quality

b) the supplier is not clearly identified

c) the consignment is inadequately identified.

Foodpro Ltd GRN No. 214/93

Date: 27/5/93   **Unloaded by**: JB   **Received from**: ICI Northwich

Carrier: Own   **Vehicle No**: DHS24J   **Delivery note No.** 7789

Description of goods   **No. of packages,**   **Weight or quantity**

Common salt, food grade 20 x 50 kg

Inspection outcome: **Accepted to store**: Yes

Question 5

The excerpt overleaf from the label of a drum of edible oil supplied by Foodpro fails to conform to BS 5750 because:

a) traceability marking is inadequate

b) insufficient indication of shelf life is provided

c) the product net weight is given in kilogrammes and not pounds.

Foodpro Limited

Question 5 continued

Sunflower oil, edible

275 kg net

Best before: 31.10.93   **Batch number:**

Quality approved by: JC

Store in a cool place.

Question 6

The undernoted specimen HOLD label used by Foodpro to identify nonconforming product fails to conform to BS 5750 because:

a) its purpose is not clear

b) the incident is not clearly traceable to a register of quarantined goods

c) responsibility for eventual disposition of the goods is unclear.

Held under quarantine

Product : Canned steak in gravy; 300 g size

Date quarantined: 21.4.93

Reference number:

Do not use or remove label until authorised by quality manager or delegate.

Question 7

A glass hydrometer found lying on its side on a bench between readings of salt solutions could fail BS 5750 because:
a) its accuracy could be impaired by lying horizontally
b) it should be kept immersed in water to prevent 'drying out'
c) test instruments should be properly protected and stored.

Question 8

A process control thermometer is found to have slipped out of calibration on a spot check. It is immediately replaced by a formally calibrated one and scrapped. Next day the incident is written up under a corrective action procedure. This could fail BS 5750 because:
a) process thermometers should never move out of calibration
b) an immediate investigation should have been held to ascertain whether product quality had been affected
c) spot checks of calibrated instruments should not be carried out.

Question 9

A company does not bring under formal calibration pressure gauges in the steam delivery system from its boiler house. This is:
a) in breach of the calibration clause of BS 5750
b) in breach of the process control clause of BS 5750
c) acceptable provided the gauges are regularly checked for fitness for purpose.

Question 10

A stockist of a wide range of products accepts them to store on the strength of: correct quantity delivered; correct delivery note; correct label information including specification number and sound condition. This is:
a) acceptable under BS 5750
b) acceptable under BS 5750 given further assurances such as purchase from an approved source and traceability of material
c) in breach of BS 5750 for inspection of incoming goods.

Question 11

During assessment an auditor saw the undernoted handwritten notice on the wall beside a reaction vessel.

N.B. Till further notice, all product should be heated to 85 degree Centigrade before being pumped to the filling line.

This could fail BS 5750 because :
a) the notice is not of official issue because it is unsigned by an appropriate person and undated
b) handwritten instructions are not allowed under BS 5750
c) handwritten, wall mounted notices are not allowed under BS 5750.

Question 12

A micrometer under formal calibration is found to be untagged to show its calibration status. This is:
a) in breach of the calibration clause of BS 5750
b) acceptable provided its case is tagged and the instrument is traceable to a list of calibrated instruments
c) acceptable because micrometers are robust instruments which are not subject to deviation.

Question 13

During assessment to BS 5750 a fork lift truck driver is seen to be driving very fast while conveying palletised finished goods to the warehouse. Strictly in terms of BS 5750, this could fail the company because :
a) it is evidence of poor workmanship with risk of damaging product
b) it is anti-social
c) it is in breach of the *Health and Safety at Work Act*.

Question 14

The following excerpt from an internal quality audit follow up report was noticed by an assessor while inspecting a company's audit records. It would be listed as a nonconformance because:

a) the audit has not been properly 'closed out' by the auditor

b) the conclusion reached under remedial action completion report is invalid

c) the remedial action form does not trace clearly to the relevant audit.

Quality Record No 16.1.2   **Retention period**: Two years

Title: Internal quality audit noncompliance report with consequential action

Originator: QM   **Date of issue**: 1.1.93   **Issue number**: First

Audit reference number: 22 (For full details see relevant form 16.1.1)

Noncompliance: N22/1

An audit of the night shift plant cleaning/sanitisation efficiency on 10.10.93 revealed the presence of cooked food residues on the inside of the stainless steel pipe connecting vessels A and B, indicating a breakdown of the system.

Signed, auditors _____ J. Smith

Signed, auditee _____ P. White

Recommended remedial action
1   Investigate the cause of the system breakdown.
2   Consider whether there are wider implications for plant hygiene.
3   Rewrite the relevant part of the cleaning procedure if necessary.
4   Take other remedial action as may be necessary.

Target completion date 10.11.93

Signed, auditors _____ J. Smith

Signed, auditee _____ P. White

Remedial action completion report

1   The plant is automatically 'cleaned in place' by pumping of detergent and sanitiser solutions around it in a computer controlled sequence. Investigation revealed a 'lazy' valve which failed to direct sufficient detergent to the pipe connecting vessels. A and B.
2   The 'lazy' valve incident is the first of its kind. Position discussed with manufacturer who recommends greasing moving parts once a week instead of once a month. **Recommendation adopted and implemented.**
3   Plant engineer please review on a daily basis.

Signed, auditee _____ P. White

Approved (signed) by auditor _____ Date _____

Question 15

The undernoted excerpt from the minutes of a management review would be listed as a nonconformance because:

a) too much time has elapsed since the previous review

b) the range of topics reviewed is inappropriate

c) there is insufficient senior management representation at the review.

Quality Record 1.1   **Retention period**: Five years

Title: Management review record

Originator: QM   **Date of issue**: 1.6.92   **Issue number**: 1

Date of meeting: 1.10.93

Chaired by: J Smith (Managing Director);

In attendance: J Jones (Quality Manager); J Green (Production Manager); F Brown (Marketing Director); J Love and R Black, Production Shift Supervisors

1   Review of minutes of previous meeting of 1.4.92. See attached record.

2   Current business

2.1 Customer complaints review

2.2 Review of internal quality audits

2.3 Review of nonconformances

2.4 Review of corrective actions

2.5 Review of 'concessions'

2.6 Review of statistical quality control

Correct responses to the multiple choice tests

Question 1:

Response a) 'Sugar' is insufficient definition without qualification, for example, by a specification number or equivalent clarification.

Question 2:

Response c) 'Usual one' does not define the supplier adequately.

Question 3

Response a) The document is not initialled by the originator.

Question 4:

Response a) No entry has been made to indicate the inspection outcome.

Question 5:

Response a) No batch number or equivalent is stated to provide 'traceability'.

Question 6:

Response b) There is no marked reference number or equivalent to trace to a register of quarantined goods.

Question 7:

Response c) Hydrometers do not suffer from lying horizontally or not being immersed in water. They should however be racked when not in use.

Question 8:

Response b) No further comment.

Question 9:

Response c) Pressure gauges in delivery systems generally serve an indicating purpose in contrast to those situated in critical locations such as steam sterilisers.

Question 10:

Response b) In our experience this is an acceptable option given due control.

Question 11:

Response a) Temporary handwritten instructions are acceptable provided they are appropriately issued.

Question 12:

Response b) It is not practicable to tag small instruments. The alternative arrangements are satisfactory.

Question 13

Response a) (However true, b and c may also be so in their own right.)

Question 14

Response a) The simple omission of the auditor's signature or initials is a minor nonconformity.

Question 15:

Response a) The previous management review was held eighteen months earlier. A lapse of more than one year between reviews is unacceptable. Many companies hold such reviews on a quarterly or six monthly basis.

List of Third Party Assessment and Certification Bodies

Certification Body	Date of accreditation	Registration No.
Associated Offices Quality Certification Ltd Longridge House Longridge Place Manchester M60 4DT Tel: 061 833 2295 Fax: 061 833 9965	May 1990	14
ASTA Certification Services Prudential Chambers 23/24 Market Place Rugby CV21 3DU Tel: 0788 578435 Fax: 0788 573605	June 1989	10
BMT Quality Assessors Ltd Scottish Metropolitan Alpha Centre Stirling University Innovation Park Stirling FK9 4NF Tel: 0786 450891 Fax: 0786 451087	September 1992	24
BSI Quality Assurance PO Box 375 Milton Keynes MK14 6LL Tel: 0908 220908 FAx: 0908 220671	January 1987	3
British Approval Service for Electric Cables Silbury Court 360 Silbury Boulevard Milton Keynes MK9 2AF Tel: 0908 691121 Fax: 0908 692722	April 1987	4
Bureau Veritas Quality International Ltd 3rd Floor 70 Borough High Street London SE1 1XF Tel: 071 378 8113 Fax: 071 378 8014	November 1988	8

Central Certification Service Ltd Victoria House 123 Midland Road Wellingborough Northants NN8 1LU Tel: 0933 441796 Fax: 0933 440247	June 1991	18
Ceramic Industry Certification Scheme Ltd Queens Road Penkull Stoke-on-Trent ST4 7LQ Tel: 0782 411008 Fax: 0782 412331	July 1987	6
Construction Quality Assurance Ltd Arcade Chambers The Arcade, Market Place Newark Notts NG24 1UD Tel: 0636 708700 Fax: 0636 708766	July 1989	12
Det Norske Vertitas Quality Assurance Ltd Veritas House 112 Station Road Sidcup Kent DA15 7BU Tel: 081 309 7477 Fax: 081 309 5907	July 1989	13
Electrical Equipment Certification Service Health and Safety Executive Harpur Hill Buxton Derbyshire SK17 9JN Tel: 0298 26211 Fax: 0298 79514	April 1992	20
Electricity Association Quality Assurance Ltd 30 Millbank London SW1P 4RD Tel: 071 834 2333 Fax: 071 931 0356	July 1992	22
Engineering Inspection Authorities Board c/o Institution of Mechanical Engineers 1 Birdcage Walk London SW1H 9JJ Tel: 071 973 1271 Fax: 071 222 4557	June 1991	17

ISO Quality Assurance Register Limited Suite 7 Metropolitan House City Park Business Village Cornbrook Manchester M16 9HQ Tel: 061 877 6914 Fax: 061 877 6915	February 1993	26
Lloyd's Register Quality Assurance Ltd Norfolk House Wellesley Road Croydon CR9 2DT Tel: 081 688 6882/3 Fax: 081 681 8146	February 1986	1
National Approval Council for Security Systems Queensgate House 14 Cookham Road Maidenhead Berkshire SL6 8AJ Tel: 0628 37512 Fax: 0628 773367	February 1992	19
National Inspection Council Quality Assurance Ltd 5 Cotswold Business Park Millfield Lane Caddington Beds LU1 4AR Tel: 0582 841144 FAx: 0582 841288	July 1990	15
SIRA Certification Service Saighton Lane Saighton Chester CH3 6EG Tel: 0244 332200 Fax: 0244 332112	June 1989	11
SGS Yarsley International Certification Service Ltd Trowers Way Redhill Surrey RH1 2JN Tel: 0737 768445 Fax: 0737 761229	April 1987	5

Steel Construction QA Scheme Ltd 4 Whitehall Court Westminster London SW1A 2ES Tel: 071 839 8566 Fax: 071 976 1634	May 1992	21
The Loss Prevention Certification Board Ltd Melrose Avenue Boreham Wood Hertfordshire WD6 2BJ Tel: 081 207 2345 Fax: 081 207 6305	October 1988	7
The Quality Scheme for Ready Mixed Concrete 3 High Street Hampton Middlesex TW12 2SQ Tel: 081 941 0273 Fax: 081 979 4558	December 1988	9
TRADA Certification Ltd Stocking Lane Hughenden Valley High Wycombe Bucks HP14 4NR Tel: 0494 565484 Fax: 0494 565487	February 1991	16
TWI Qualification Services Abington Hall Abington Cambridge CB1 6AL Tel: 0223 891162 Fax: 0223 894219	September 1992	25
UK Certificating Authority for Reinforcing Steels Oak House Tubs Hill Sevenoaks Kent TN13 1BL Tel: 0732 450000 Fax: 0732 455917	October 1986	2
Water Industry Certification Scheme Frankland Road Blagrove Swindon Wilts SN5 8YF Tel: 0793 410005 Fax: 0793 410009	July 1992	23

Index